"TO OUR LAST MAN"

"TO OUR LAST MAN"

TONY SQUIRE

S.A.Squire & T.Squire

Contents

Dedication — vi
Cover Information — viii
Foreword — xi

1. After the fury of the storm — 1
2. Amidst the shifting sands — 18
3. There is no place to hide and so we are found — 32
4. Easy does it — 51
5. Fight like Trojans and die like Spartans — 70
6. Pluck, dash and endurance — 136
7. From shirkers to workers — 163
8. Pack up your troubles — 189
9. We'll drink a cup of kindness yet — 209
10. But not a drop to drink — 225

About The Author — 250
More Books By This Author — 251

I dedicate this book to all who have served in the armed forces, whether in a combat or support arm, each person being part of a well oiled machine, each dependent on one another. When you were needed you were ready. Let no man put asunder.

Copyright © 2024 by TONY SQUIRE

All rights reserved.

Some of the characters and events portrayed in this book are based on real people and events from history, whilst others, including spoken word, are fictitious. Any similarity to real persons, living or dead, is coincidental and not intended by the author.

No part of this book may be reproduced in any manner whatsoever without written permission except in the case of brief quotations embodied in critical articles and reviews.

First Printing, 2024

Cover Information

Cover design by Tony Squire.

Cover Photographs are courtesy of the Australian War Memorial, Canberra.

Front Cover (Top):

Accession Number – E00019.
Maker – Herbert Frederick Baldwin.
Place Made - France: Picardie, Somme, Albert Combles Area, Montauban.

Australian War Memorial Description - Unidentified men of the 5th Division partaking in cigarettes and resting by the side of the Montauban road, near Mametz, while enroute to the trenches. Most of the men are wearing sheepskin jackets and woollen gloves and are carrying full kit and .303 Lee Enfield rifles.

Copyright – Item copyright: Copyright expired: Public Domain.

Front Cover (Bottom):

Accession Number – B01450.
Maker – James Francis (Frank) Hurley.
Place Made – Ottoman Empire, Palestine.

Australian War Memorial Description - The 1st Australian Light Horse Brigade moving down from Judea to the capture of Jericho. Brigadier General Cox is at the head of the column, with Major A Chisholme DSO (Brigade Major), next to him.

Copyright – Item copyright: Copyright expired: Public Domain.

Rear Cover:

Accession Number – EZ0098.
Maker - British Official Photographer.
Place Made - France: Picardie, Somme, Albert Bapaume Area, Pozieres Area, Pozieres.

Australian War Memorial Description - An Australian fatigue party from the 7th Brigade (far left) carrying piles of empty sandbags to the front line through the devastated area near Pozieres. The structure on the left is the remains of a German observation post, which stood on the western end of the village and was nicknamed 'Gibraltar' by the Australians. The post consisted of a concrete covered stairway down to a cellar from a house that formerly stood on the site and a larger, excavated chamber, and the whole housed three officers and 23 men. The occupants surrendered to a party from the 2nd Battalion on 23 July 1916 during the battle to wrest Pozieres from the Germans. Between 23 July and early September, the 1st, 2nd and 4th Divisions between them launched 19 attacks on German positions in and around the ruins of Pozieres.

Copyright – Item copyright: Copyright expired: Public Domain.

Foreword

As I mentioned in my first novel in the ANZAC Chronicles, I still find it perplexing why the school curriculum teaches so little about the Great War and the ANZACs. We seem to know almost nothing about the numerous regiments formed during the war or that approximately eight to ten percent of the country's population at the time volunteered to fight. Yes, they volunteered - there was no conscription in Australia.

When it comes to the battles they fought, most people are familiar with Gallipoli, the Somme, and the charge of the Light Horse at Beersheba. But how many can say they know about the battles of Pozieres, Mouquet Farm, Romani, Magdhaba, and Magruntein? Not many, which is why my novels focus on two Queensland regiments, the 9th Battalion and the 2nd Light Horse Regiment. You may or may not have heard of them; they didn't participate in all the famous battles, but they were involved in some. Through my fictional characters, Archie, Percy, and Rueben Taylor, my books aim to bring the Great War to life.

In the first novel of the series, "...UNTIL YOU ARE SAFE," the Taylor boys enlist in 1914, and we follow their training in Australia, Egypt, and Lemnos before they move on to Gallipoli. In this second novel, set in 1916, the boys and their friends part ways - Percy and the 2nd Light Horse stay in the Middle East, while Archie and Rueben, with the 9th Battalion, head to the Western Front.

Though my main characters are fictional, their units and the events described are real. For my research, I relied on two remarkable books: "History of the 2nd Light Horse Regiment A.I.F. – 1914-1919" by Lieutenant Colonel G.H. Bourne, DSO, and "From ANZAC to the Hindenburg Line – The History of the 9th Battalion A.I.F." by Norman K. Harvey, BA, AACI. These invaluable accounts, written by those who were there, provide incredible insights into the regiments' formation, trials, and eventual return.

In my novels, I strive to mention actual soldiers from these units whenever possible, often featuring my fictional characters alongside real individuals on specific missions. One prominent figure I highlighted this time is Private John Leak, the only member of the 9th Battalion to be awarded the Victoria Cross during the Great War. While my characters accompany him, the glory remains solely his, as it should. The battles, dates, and locations in my novel are authentic, and I believe my descriptions convey how challenging a soldier's life was at the turn of the twentieth century, relying mostly on foot travel or, for the Light Horse, their mounts.

I hope I have done justice to their stories and look forward to shedding more light on them in future novels in the series.

I

After the fury of the storm

Blackness. Winter. A night of warm breezes and no moon.

As the troopship floated on the calm Mediterranean Sea, beyond the ship's high bow those who had ventured out early on deck could see the stars and lights of Alexandria reflecting on the shimmering water. The Mediterranean was fed by the Atlantic Ocean and the various rivers and streams which trickled from the desert landscape in the dry summer, but which now flowed fast and frothing as they met the open sea. The mighty River

Nile, which cut a path through the flat and fertile farmland along its banks, foamed along, filling the irrigation channels to its sides before meeting the distant sea.

The 2nd Light Horse Regiment had been encamped on East Mudros following the evacuation from Gallipoli, and had embarked on the 'Ionan' on the 22nd of December 1915, departing Mudros at midnight. Arriving at Alexandria five days later, having spent their second Christmas of the war at sea, was a relief for all.

As the convoy of ships glided into the harbour, the skyline of the ancient city unfolded before the eyes of the arriving soldiers. The sights before them seemed a stark contrast to the tranquil beauty of the harbour. Despite the picturesque setting and the evident historical significance of the place, their arrival brought a sobering realisation that, for them, little had changed, except for a temporary reprieve from the battlefield. Instead of grandeur, they were greeted by the same dirty, hay-strewn wharf and drab office buildings that they had seen the last time they were here. Life here had gone on as usual, without a second thought for these, now battle weary, men who had endured so much to keep the people of Egypt safe from the Turks. As the men scrambled out on deck, to take in the sights and breathe in the fresh, salty air, the bustling wharf below was a hive of activity, with workers scurrying to and fro, loading and unloading cargo, while the air echoed with the sounds of seagulls and the dreaded shouts of "Australia, Australia!" from the Arab street sellers.

As Trooper "Boggy" Marsh, arms outstretched in the breeze, inhaled deeply, he was soon coughing and spluttering, his face contorted as, feeling annoyed, he reacted to the stench he was breathing in.

"Flamin' Nora!" he exclaimed, "I forgot how much this place bloody stinks".

"Never mind that mate, look at the bloody gyppos waiting for us again," replied Percy, as he observed the hordes of hawkers and pedlars congregated on the wharf.

"Well, they aint getting any of my dosh," announced Davo.

"Too bloody right," said Percy, nodding in agreement, whilst waving his arms frantically and shouting at the crowds below, "imshee! Imshee you bastards!"

As the three mates stood at the railing, fixated on the chaotic scene below, the Arab hawkers weaved through the soldiers and civilians working on the wharf, their persistent calls echoing faintly across the water, and disturbing those who were trying to earn an honest day's living.

Davo nudged Boggy, and pointed downwards where a solitary figure stood amidst the crowd. It took them a moment to recognise the familiar silhouette, the unmistakable stance of their mate, Chugger, who had been wounded back in August during the attempted Gallipoli breakout.

"Percy, look!" Davo exclaimed, "I think that's Chugger down there!"

A mixture of relief and excitement rippled through them as they realised it was indeed Chugger, standing there amidst the chaos of the wharf, pushing and slapping the hawkers away.

The boys shouted and whistled insults to their mate, as they waved vigorously at him, hoping to catch his eye.

"Oy! Chugger you old malingerer!" shouted Boggy.

A two fingered salute from Chugger indicated that he could see and hear them, as a broad smile stretched across his face, almost making it ache with happiness.

"ALL RANKS PREPARE TO DISEMBARK. PREPARE TO DISEMBARK," came the call from bridge.

"Chugger!" shouted Percy, "see you in a tick".

As Percy, Davo, and Boggy descended the gangplank, they were immediately enveloped by the Arab hawkers, who jostled for attention, their voices blending with the sounds of ship horns and seagulls overhead. But, with determined strides, the trio pushed their way through the crowd, waving off the persistent hawkers with practised ease.

"Just like the good old days eh boys?" laughed Percy.

"Stuff this!" growled Boggy, "give me a machine gun blast at Gallipoli any day mate. Now where did Chugger get to?"

As their eyes scanned the chaotic scene, they finally spotted their mate still battling with the annoying salesmen.

"Chugger!" Davo called out, his voice cutting through the noise of the crowd.

Chugger turned, his face breaking into a wide grin as he made his way towards his mates, dodging past crates and barrels as he went.

As they met for the first time in months, the atmosphere was a mixture of excitement and relief, handshakes turning into hearty embraces, as the four friends reunited amidst the hustle and bustle of Alexandria.

"How are yer mate?" asked Percy.

"I'm good mate...as good as new," replied Chugger as he managed a quick twirl, "see?"

"That *is* good news. We missed you mate," replied Percy.

"Hey, how did the evacuation go? Have you heard from Archie and the boys in the ninth?" Chugger enquired.

"We saw Archie, Roo and the fellas for a couple of days before we left. They came back to help with the withdrawal and final defence," Percy replied, "and you'll never guess who is a sergeant major?"

Chugger stood shrugging his shoulders and waiting for Percy to reply to his own question.

"Well? Come on then...I'm not one of those fortune teller people you know?" said Chugger.

"Clancy bloody McBride..." announced Percy.

"Nooo...well you've got to admit he *is* a bloody good soldier," replied Chugger, smiling to himself and scratching his head, "Clancy McBride eh? A man of me own heart. Anyway, how did leaving Gallipoli go?"

"I'm glad to say that we got off without a scratch, and the lack of news suggests that Arch, Roo and the boys did the same," replied Percy, "but it seems marvellous when you think of it. Old Jacko knew nothing of what we were up to, but if he *had* known and rushed us, not a man would have got off".

"What a bloody marvel," said Chugger, "I hope you left him a few parting gifts".

"We sure did," said Boggy.

A shout from the sergeant major announced that it was time to fall in and move out to camp.

As the men formed up Percy quickly whispered to Chugger.

"Hey Chug. Where are we off to?"

"Heliopolis mate," replied Chugger.

Unlike their previous camp at Ma'adi, prior to leaving for Lemnos, Heliopolis was one of the oldest cities of ancient Egypt, but was now in a sorry state, its temples and other buildings having been scavenged for the construction of Cairo during medieval times. The land, however, was flat, and nearby was the base of the Royal Flying Corps at Aerodrome Camp.

On arrival, the regiment settled in to their tented lines, which had been constructed, and neatly laid out, by their comrades who had been wounded on the peninsula and were now back to good health and fitness. All of the men were excited to see their horses again and get back in the saddle, but in the mean time there were a few surprises; mail, and Christmas Billies from home.

The soldiers were very pleased to receive their Christmas presents from Australia, which had been sent through an organisation called the War Chest. Every man in the regiment was presented with a billy can which contained a myriad of gifts; a plum pudding, a Canterbury cake, a pound of chocolate, a tin of sweets, a pipe, cigarettes, tobacco, a shirt, a good pair of socks, a woollen scarf, writing paper, and all manner of other items.

Chugger was particularly pleased, and suddenly became very popular, when he discovered that the lady volunteer who had packed *his* billy had slipped in a very nice bottle of brandy.

"Just the ticket..."

Each man felt extremely lucky, like a mob of children who had just received their Christmas stockings, but there was a deeper feeling, one of not being forgotten by the people of Australia. They were indeed blessed and fully appreciated such nice things after months of a diet of bully beef and biscuits.

Percy and the boys had also been inundated with letters and parcels from home, which had finally caught up with them via Gallipoli and Lemnos.

"Look at this boys," laughed Percy as he proudly displayed his haul of letters and parcels, "six letters from Lil, and just look at this picture of Frank...look how big he is...gosh I miss him and Lil...and look, a jumper and socks from mum and dad".

Boggy gazed over at Percy expectantly.

"That's all nice, but..." he paused, "is there any cake?"

"You cheeky bugger," replied Percy as he reached in to one of the packages, produced a tin, and tossed it to Boggy, "here you go...cut yourself a slice, pass it round...but make sure I get some or there'll be hell to pay".

"You bloody beauty!" exclaimed Chugger, licking his lips, "you can always rely on Doris".

As the boys sat in the sun, enjoying reading their mail, not far from them was an irrigation channel, and about one hundred yards away some Egyptians were watering a herd of sheep; the whole scene, with the native Egyptians clothed as they were, presenting a picture of biblical times. On the opposite bank date palms grew luxuriantly, whilst awkward looking wooden boats carried cargoes up and down the channel. It was a far cry from the turbulent months on Gallipoli; but the war was not over yet. For the ANZACs a new phase was just beginning.

Towards the close of 1915, German agents had been stirring up unrest amongst the Senouissi Arabs of Western Egypt. This belligerent tribe were a constant threat to the Nile Valley, and this fact was being milked expertly by the enemy. To assist in protecting upper and western Egypt a sizeable force had been maintained and, on their return from the Dardanelles, the 1st Light Horse Brigade was attached to it.

The first order of the day for the 2nd Light Horse Regiment was re-organisation and promotions.

The Commanding Officer, Lieutenant Colonel Glasgow was given command of the 13th Infantry Brigade and took with him Captain Steele and several newly commissioned Senior Non Commissioned Officers (SNCOs). Each man was highly respected, and the regiment felt their loss deeply. Another popular promotion and appointment was the newly promoted Major General Harry Chauvel who was now the Commander of the ANZAC Mounted Division.

"So, who's our CO *now* then?" asked Boggy.

"A Major Barlow; from the 11th Regiment. I hear he's a good bloke," replied Percy.

After months away at Gallipoli, separated from their beloved horses, the soldiers finally reunited with their loyal steeds, and eagerly saddled up once more. The sensation of the Lighthorsemen finally returning to their saddles was one of relief and familiarity. It was as though they were reuniting with old friends after a long absence; which they were. The weight of the saddle, the feel of the reins in their hands, and the rhythmic movement of their horse beneath them brought a sense of comfort and purpose that had been absent during their time away.

The weather on Lemnos in late December had been bitterly cold, soap was a scarce commodity, and most of the men were without razors, having left them on Gallipoli. The 9th Battalion's

Commanding Officer was a practical and thoughtful man, and as the battalion were originally on Lemnos for a rest, before returning to the peninsula, he had conferred with the Medial Officer, Doc Butler, who informed him that beards were a great protection for the face and throat. Ever one for uniformity within the battalion, the colonel issued an order that all ranks should cease shaving and allow their beards to grow. Other units who had not been placed on similar orders soon christened the battalion the "Hairy 9th" or the "Bearded 9th", which soon became the "Beery 9th".

When Archie and the boys arrived back on the island following the final evacuation of Gallipoli, they couldn't believe what they were seeing.

"Stone the flamin' crows!" Clancy exclaimed, "I know it's almost Christmas but this takes the biscuit".

"Yeah, it's like being in a battalion full of Father Christmases," Roo agreed as they surveyed the scruffy, unkempt sights of beards of all lengths, colours and descriptions.

But the arrival of the Gallipoli rear guard signalled a return to normality, and the non-shaving order was cancelled.

It would soon be time for the troops to return to Egypt, with Christmas Eve being set for the day of departure. However, this was cancelled at short notice and Christmas Day granted as a holiday.

Just like the soldiers in Egypt, the troops on Lemnos were also issued with Christmas Billies.

"We could have used these on Gallipoli," Clancy observed, as he wrapped his new woollen scarf around his neck.

"I wonder when we are off to Egypt?" Roo enquired, "It would be good to see Percy and the fellas again".

"Well chaps," interrupted Ponsonby, "between you, me and the gate post the brigade headquarters is departing tomorrow".

"That was quick. No rest for us rear party blokes then eh?" groaned Archie.

"Cheer up, there will be ample relaxation time once we get back to Egypt," Ponsonby reassured the men.

"Yeah right," added Clancy, "is that *before* or after we *build* our camp?"

"Yes, there does seem to be a lot of disorganisation on that account, but I'm sure things have improved," replied a hopeful Ponsonby.

On the 30th of December 1915, the battalion received definite orders to move to Egypt and would sail aboard the 'Grampian', along with other units. On this day the battalion strength was twenty two officers and six hundred and eighty nine other ranks, which made the total on board ship around seventeen hundred men. There was always something sad in the departure of a ship, increasing when that vessel was a transport conveying soldiers who expect to face death. But at 0800 hours on the first day of 1916, the ship sailed *away* from danger, to Alexandria, and although, throughout its three day journey, the ship was under threat of attack from German submarines, *that* particular thought was far from the minds of these battle hardened veterans of Gallipoli.

At about 0850 hours on the 3rd of January the 'Grampian'

passed through the entrance to Alexandria Harbour, just as the lighthorsemen had, less than a week earlier. As the troops on deck watched the familiar sights of the port, they pondered over the last time they were there.

"I can't believe it's been nearly eleven months since we sailed off to ANZAC, or should I say Lemnos *then* ANZAC," remarked Archie'.

"The place hasn't changed a bit," added Taff.

"Yeah, it still bloody stinks like an overflowing dunny!" said Clancy.

Tel-El-Kebir was the battalion's ultimate destination, situated thirty five miles west of the Suez Canal and seventy miles from Cairo. The troops disembarked from the ship in the early evening and were soon surrounded by hordes of pedlars, hawkers and boot blacks.

"Bloody hell, give me Gallipoli any day boys," shouted Clancy as he pushed and punched his way through the bustling gyppo salesmen.

Once on board their train, the men were relatively safe from the enterprising and annoying traders.

"No doubt there'll be more of the buggers at the other end," sighed Taff.

"Yeah, well the bastards will be feeling the toe of my boot then won't they?!" exclaimed Clancy.

As the train passed through the desert landscape some men took the advantage and slept, whilst others gazed at the barren countryside.

"Did you know that there was a big battle where we're going;

about twenty six years ago?" said Archie, "The Tommies beat the Egyptian rebels or something".

"Shame they didn't teach the bastards some manners!" added Clancy.

The weather during their journey quickly changed from sunny to constant, heavy rain. The first train arrived at Tel-El-Kebir at 1300 hours. The new camp was only a short march away, and was a barren place.

"Bugger me! I'll have a question asked in parliament!" growled Clancy, "no bloody anything! Again!"

"Skipper, where's the camp? The tents?" asked Roo, "it's Mena and Lemnos all over again!"

"Sorry Roo," replied Ponsonby, "I have no idea, and am just as disappointed as all of you".

After his initial moan and groan, Clancy very quickly got himself into Sergeant Major mode, informing the troops of their dilemma and instructing them to do their best to get comfy and keep dry. Guards were mounted and the routine of sleep commenced.

The previous day's heavy downpour had acted like a curtain, but as dawn broke, the daylight revealed a sparse and vast dry landscape.

"It's like Gallipoli, only flat," observed Taff.

For the moment the 9th were the first occupants, so in their companies, platoons and sections, set about constructing the new camp. Tents and other materials were scarce, but the battalion laid down 'streets', which were designated by rock borders, and set out lines for any battalions which may come later. Clancy was in his element and had become quite the organiser.

"I think you're enjoying this sergeant major," remarked Ponsonby.

"After Gallipoli mate I think a bit of organisation will go a long way to raising the morale of these blokes. Not that they need it, but a few comforts are always a good thing eh?" said Clancy.

"Exactly...that's the spirit. Well said Clancy," said Ponsonby, "I think you are taking to your new role like a duck to water old boy".

The men were kept occupied and were relieved that they weren't just sitting round twiddling their thumbs. However, disgust, disbelief and humiliation were the feelings around camp on the 5th of January when those in higher authority decreed that these veterans of Gallipoli, for some unknown reason, required brushing up on their ceremonial drill...saluting by numbers and all that.

Clancy, who was usually outspoken, for once could not argue or voice an opinion on the matter, for he was now the Company Sergeant Major, having arrived on the peninsula as a Private soldier and leaving as a Warrant Officer Class Two. He was a good soldier, of that no one doubted, but an instructor of Drill he was not. Luckily, his old master, Sergeant MacDonald, was, and he very kindly offered his services...perhaps too eagerly. But, as Clancy McBride soon discovered, delegation was part of his job and, in this case, he was more than happy to oblige and oversee the whole fiasco.

"Come on sarge, we did all this back in Brissie," came a disgruntled voice from the ranks.

Big Sergeant Mac was not a happy man at being referred to as Sarge.

"Listen here you wee beasties, there are two types of sarge, that's a saus...arge and a mass...arge; and if any of you wee dobbers call me that again you'll be getting a discharge...after the war of course," he shouted.

"Well...I aint doin' it!" came another voice.

The sergeant could see that this was not going to be an easy task and began searching the ranks for a familiar face.

"Private Jackson are you here laddy?" he called.

"Sergeant!" shouted Jacko as he snapped smartly to attention.

"Jacko, are these here gentlemen aware of how I helped yer overcome yer fear of sailing?" asked the sergeant.

Jacko remembered how he had panicked on the gang plank at Pinkenba in 1914, followed by the sudden blow from Sergeant Mac, then waking up on the troop ship out at sea. He placed his hand on his jaw, just on the spot on which he had been struck.

There was silence, followed by murmurs from the ranks.

"I think they are, yes, sergeant," replied Jacko.

"Well then laddies, enough said. Let's get to it shall we?" replied Mac, with a glint in his eye.

Punch one and train a thousand was Mac's philosophy and, not wanting to feel the wrath of the big Scotsman, the men quickly relented, dispelled any rebellious thoughts, and commenced their ceremonial refresher training.

Lieutenant Ponsonby, standing with the CSM, was very pleased.

"Sergeant Mac is a damned good fellow," announced the officer.

"He is sir," replied Clancy, feeling contemplative.

Ponsonby noticed an unusual quietness in the CSM.

"What is it Clancy? You seem a little thoughtful at the moment," asked Ponsonby.

The sergeant major turned to his friend.

"Well mate, I'm just wondering why I'm the sergeant major and not Mac there?" replied Clancy.

"To be honest he *was* the first choice, but he recommended you. Says he saw a bit of Jacobite spirit in you. Must be the name McBride," Ponsonby answered.

"Really?!" exclaimed Clancy, casting a glance towards the sergeant, "that was very good of him".

The CSM observed the drill practice with renewed vigour and admiration for Sergeant MacDonald.

As the men were marched off the square, after performing well for their sergeant, Clancy shouted out to them.

"Good work boys. I think you deserve a treat".

"Beer?" shouted one hopeful soldier.

"The mail is in...one hundred and fifty bags of it...Taff, maybe even *you've* got some mate!" teased Clancy.

As he swung his arms to the front and rear, Taff managed a sly two fingered salute to the CSM.

"I saw that you bludger!" laughed the CSM, which was followed by a few laughs from the company as they marched towards the battalion lines.

Archie and Roo, now platoon sergeants, distributed the long awaited post to the troops. Sitting round their camp fires each man was engrossed in their news from home. Doris had sent her usual biscuits and cakes to Archie, Roo and Clancy, but this time each received a photograph.

"Hey, look Clance, this is mum, dad, Lil and little Frank…my, he's grown," said Archie.

"I've got one too mate," replied Clancy, feeling blessed.

"You're part of the family now mate," announced Roo.

"Your mum says they've built a room just for me in the barn," said Clancy, as a tear came to his eye.

Roo stood up, sat next to his mate, and gently placed his arm around Clancy's shoulders.

"We're brothers mate, and don't you forget it," said Roo.

As Clancy wiped his eyes he reached into his pocket, pulled out his wallet, and placed the photograph inside.

"I'll keep this close to my heart boys," said Clancy, his voice quivering.

"Mum reckons they might build some more rooms cos she has a feeling that we might bring more new family members home with us," said Archie.

"Your mum and dad are real gooduns boys," replied Clancy.

The next day, Lieutenant Carroll arrived with re-enforcements in tow, bringing the battalion's strength up to nine hundred and thirty six.

Even though the ages of the new men ranged from early twenties to mid forties, compared to the veterans they all looked like fresh faced school boys. The original 9th Battalion men seemed older and wiser after all that they had been through.

The new men were distributed around the battalion. 'B' Company received Private Jeremy Kropp, a boisterous young lad from Toogoolawah. He had an opinion about, and knew, everything...well, according to himself anyway. That said, each new arrival was in awe of the old guard, and were disappointed that they had arrived too late for the Dardanelles campaign.

Clancy was concerned about the company's latest recruit and confided with Archie and Roo.

"Keep an eye on that Kropp kid, he needs knocking down a peg or two".

As well as drill, military training in all subjects began in earnest, with the new tactics learned in 1915, being added to the syllabus, but the reason for the ceremonial drill practice finally became apparent on the 15th of January when the 1st Division was reviewed by General Sir Archibald Murray, the new Commander In Chief of the troops in this area.

Regimental Sergeant Major Ruddle and his CSMs had put in a lot of work reorganising and smartening up the battalion. Although strict, the RSM was liked by all and, to his credit, the battalion was now a very professional and well oiled machine.

2

Amidst the shifting sands

On the 25th of January the battalion was ordered to the Suez Canal, and at 2000 hours the 9th boarded a train to Serapeum, eight miles south of Ismailia. They arrived at around 2300 hours and set up bivvies during an extremely cold night, and, after an early reveille, the 9th Battalion crossed the canal by ferry at 0600 hours the next morning, then marched to a very sandy desert camp approximately a mile eastwards.

On the 27th, 'A' and 'B' Companies, under Major Salisbury,

moved out at 0830 hours and marched nine miles to Gebel Habeita, where they set up a defensive position. The remaining companies arrived the next day.

The battalion had been deployed in order to deny the Turks a direct attack route to the canal, but due to the heat, poor supply lines, and terrain, they were having a bad time of it.

Digging trenches was made difficult due to the continual collapsing of the sandy walls, however, Clancy had his CSM head on and directed the troops to fill sand bags and use them to construct the internal trench walls. For the trench it was a success, but the strong desert winds blew enough sand in to the air to half fill any trench in its path. Soldier's blankets and uniform which had been laid out to dry would also be buried, making it difficult for the owners to locate their property.

The food and water ration too was pretty bad; bully beef and a meagre water supply per day.

The troops were not impressed!

"This is no way to fight a war!" was the general consensus.

After a week of misery, grumbling and making do, the full water supply, fresh meat and milk, began to arrive on a daily basis, courtesy of the Royal Engineers who had laid a light railway from the canal to a position half way distant.

Being in a defensive position, however, did not alter some of the ridiculous decisions being made at Brigade level. On his inspection of the defences on the 5th of February, the Brigadier ordered that ceremonial drill be carried out by all for half an hour each day. That decision went down well.

"At this rate we will not only look good but will be able to kill Abdul by numbers!" exclaimed Stowie.

There was, however, a reprieve for some when an outbreak of mumps resulted in many being evacuated to hospital. Morale was not at its greatest at this time until the Quartermaster used £100 from battalion funds in order to purchase luxuries for the canteen. Needless to say, the canteen sold out in just a few hours.

The battalion now began to patrol in earnest, with daily patrols being sent out to a distance of thirty miles. The good news for the men was that their feet would be spared, courtesy of attached Indian soldiers from the Bikanir Camel Corps, plus their forty camels. The patrols not only broke the monotony for the soldiers, but also were a chance to barter with their new Indian mates for spices to liven up their bland rations.

The majority of the men could ride a horse, so, after a quick lesson, the troops moved out with the confidence of Lighthorsemen...or so they thought.

As they rode through the seemingly endless sandpit, the sun cast elongated shadows of their camels against the many dunes, making them appear like giants riding domesticated dinosaurs. The troops were feeling pretty high and mighty right now, travelling in a camel caravan through the sands of the desert, led by their trusty Indian guides, silent and stoic figures to a man, draped in khaki and crowned with turbans. But it wasn't so easy, as camels have a particular style of walking that's perfect for the loose sandy desert environment, but less than perfect for your posterior, so for the infantrymen every shifting minute on the dunes was a minute too long, and some of the troops were in pain.

"Blimey!" exclaimed Stowie, "we've not long left the possie, yet

I'm already uncomfortable, and if I had a grain of sand for every time I've shifted sitting positions, I could fill an hour glass".

"Uncomfortable isn't the word," replied Archie, "this constant rocking up and down is making my trousers ride up and disappear up you know where!"

"Do you mean its making your bum sore mate?" laughed Clancy.

"Yeah, well, there is that too," replied a slightly sheepish Archie.

The Indian soldiers could see the difficulties the Aussies were having and rode up and down the column encouraging the men to move *with* the camel and not against it, for the less tension they held in their bodies, the more comfortable the ride. The Aussies soon got the hang of it and enjoyed their rest from foot slogging through uneven and unfriendly terrain.

On the 15th of February it was revealed that the Australian Imperial Force was to be increased in size by two new Divisions. In order to accomplish this and create thirty two battalions from the existing sixteen, General Birdwood had decided that the original battalions would lose half of their strength to make up the new units, and each battalion would be brought up to strength with the new volunteers from Australia; thus ensuring that each battalion consisted of fifty per cent veterans.

The men respected Birdy and, although no one wanted to leave their battalion families, each man could see the sense in the General's plan.

Battalion lists of those staying and departing were drawn up.

The boys of 'B' Company were tense. They wanted to remain with the 9th and certainly did not want to lose anyone to the new units. The new battalion being created from the 9th was to be the 49th Battalion.

"At least it's got a nine in it boys," announced Stowie, as he spied the CSM striding towards the group, with the Platoon Commander about twenty yards to the rear in his wake, "look out, here comes trouble"

The CSM had a broad smile on his face as he made a quick announcement.

"Hey fellas…we're staying with the 9th".

"Who is?" asked Roo.

"Me, you, Mac, Archie, Stowie, Taff, Jacko and young Kroppy here," replied Clancy.

"Ripper!" exclaimed Archie as he reached out and shook the hands of all present.

"We've got a new OC though," said Clancy, a worried expression covering his face.

The men quietly groaned and murmured to themselves and shook their heads.

"He'd better be good," Stowie piped up.

"I *am*…even if I say so myself," said Ponsonby as he arrived at the unofficial meeting, sporting his new rank of Captain.

"Bloody hell…Captain Freddy," said Archie as he offered his hand to the officer, "well done mate".

"Yeah, good on yer sir," added Stowie.

"Thank you chaps," said a grateful Freddy as he nodded acknowledgement to his friends.

"We're like the three musketeers; except there's nine of us," said Archie.

"The three what?" asked Clancy, "hasn't someone said that before?"

"Never mind mate. We're just together, that's all that counts," replied Roo.

Meanwhile, a couple of days earlier, on the 13th of February, the 2nd Light Horse Regiment had saddled up and moved out to Minia, dubbed by the locals as the "Bride of Upper Egypt", referring to its strategic location in Middle Egypt as a vital link between the north and south. It made sense that if the local population were aware of this, so were the Turks. From the 18th of February the regiment was distributed to patrol the many towns and localities. 'C' Squadron, under Major Chambers, was given the responsibility for the town of Tukh-el-Kheil. Patrols were carried out daily, hampered frequently by the Khamseens; the dry, hot winds that blew in from the desert, bringing with them an oppressive heat.

The heat, however, was not the only issue, for the load that a Lighthorseman and his horse carried in the field was substantial; the minimum load, consisting of only the bare essentials.

The Lighthorseman himself wore a leather bandolier with one hundred and fifty rounds of ammunition, a bayonet, a Lee Enfield service rifle, and a haversack typically filled with tins of bully beef and hard tack army biscuits. The horse's gear included a headstall and bridle, head rope, picketing rope, saddle, and blanket. Additionally, a leather sand muzzle was slung around the horse's neck, this muzzle, used in place of the nosebag after the horse's meagre feed, preventing it from eating sand and dirt, a bad habit which many hungry horses quickly developed. In this sand muzzle, the trooper often carried his mess-tin, or a billy for cooking or making tea, and a dandy brush for grooming. The horse also wore a bandolier around its neck containing an additional ninety rounds of ammunition. On the front of the saddle, two leather wallets held a towel, soap, spare shirt, socks, and any extra rations the rider couldn't fit into his haversack. Whilst strapped on top of these wallets were a greatcoat and one blanket.

Typically, the men set out with forty eight hours' worth of rations and an iron ration, while the horse carried twenty seven pounds of feed, enough for three days. This horse feed was divided between two nosebags tied to the saddle and a sandbag, which often had a ground or bivouac sheet rolled around it and strapped across the rear of the saddle. Also attached to the saddle were a water bottle for the soldier's own use, and a canvas water bucket for watering the horse. In some areas, where water was usually more available, each man carried two or three water bottles.

The men themselves were a pretty scraggy and lean lot, when they had first arrived back in Egypt, but had made up for it since and were now all in the best of condition. Day after day they were in the saddle from dawn to dusk, leading a roving life much like the native inhabitants of these great sandy wastes. The terrain was vast, but one view of it was much like the other, and for the most part they could look north, south, east, and west, and see nothing but vast undulating plains of gleaming sand. When they were not on the move, their nights were pretty well taken up with outposts (OPs), patrols and the like; the lonely, silent rides causing each man to get quite accustomed to his own company. Their foe did everything with lightning speed, so there was never a moment when the men weren't armed; awake or sleeping, their weapons and equipment were constantly within easy reach. Their horses and saddlery, too, were always kept in a state of absolute readiness, so that in case of alarm they could be mounted and into action in a few minutes. Except for the occasional bursts of excitement in the way of the morning and evening stand-to, the lives of the lighthorsemen were very monotonous. They were generally on the move, and the country which they traversed contained no vestige of variety, with every camp ground exactly like the last. The soldiers soon adapted themselves to the circumstances and the lazy Egyptian sunshine had its advantages, especially when a man became accustomed to solitude, sitting loosely in the saddle accompanied by thoughts of home. It was pleasant to ride and drone away the day in the peace of the open landscape, and a Trooper soon came to value the company of his horse, there being an affinity between them, which was not present under ordinary circumstances. No man who had eaten his midday ration in the desert would ever forget the shimmering heat that could be seen as well as felt, and the intense silence that would be broken only by the rhythmic munch, munch of his horse beside him.

Occasionally the column would pass through villages, which were surrounded by water for the most part, or else protected by a wall around their circumference. Most of the houses were made from mud bricks, but those belonging to the Sheiks, or holy men, and the mosques, were of stone. The stench was abominable, sanitation being completely unknown, and in many cases the livestock lived in the houses with the people. Along some routes there were a number of single residences which were constructed from bamboo and bushes, with one side left open. They would be about ten feet square and five feet high and horribly filthy people inhabited them, with the poultry, household donkey, or buffalo, as often as not occupying part of the dwelling.

The patrols were undertaken in good time with up to eleven miles being completed in three hours, with three ten minute halts. Along the way hundreds of locals would gather to watch the strange looking soldiers, and most of them would have something to sell from "tomato, big one," to "Nestless chocklate" and "Cairo kek". Very often the Arab men would be fishing in the canals, catching some nice, though small, bream and eels, which for a few pennies would make a good meal for the soldiers at the end of the day.

Most of the women would be dressed in black, and had black veils over the lower part of their faces, with a yellow piece of wood covering the nose, so that only the eyes were visible. The Aussie soldiers were always in disbelief at this sight, and were disgusted in the way that the Arabs held no value for their women folk.

"Mum would be spewing if she saw how these women are treated," remarked Percy.

"I reckon there would be a few blokes with black eyes round here eh?" added Chugger.

"I don't reckon anything has changed here since the time of

Moses," said Davo, "just look at them. They are poor and filthy, and dress just like the pictures you see in the Bible".

Boggy, feeling the mood to be a little depressing, suggested he sing a hymn, but this was met with shouts of "bloody hell mate we're downhearted already".

Much chuckling rippled through the ranks as the lighthorsemen rode on.

The 26th of February saw the quota for the 49th Battalion march out to Serapeum. None were happy about the move to form a new battalion.

A few days later a new draft of re-enforcements arrived to bolster the remaining four hundred veterans of the 9th Battalion. Not much thought or planning had gone in to the new arrivals who, it was intended, were to learn from those in the know, now experienced in the ways of warfare. Many of the new men were found to be medically unfit and, to add to the situation, they had reported with few or no weapons, and were lacking in other essential kit. To make it worse, there was no spare weaponry or equipment in the battalion stores to give to them.

Having been camped previously at Heliopolis, and experienced the 'delights' of Cairo, some of the new men were a little unruly, to put it politely.

Clancy, being the CSM, was not a happy man and promptly held a parade for their new mates. Curious, the original battalion men gathered on the edge of the parade square, eager to hear the sergeant major's words.

"PARADE...PARADE...SHUN!!" shouted Clancy as he brought the unruly mob to attention.

Ordinarily the troops would be stood at ease to hear the CSM's speech; but not today.

"Right you blokes, my name is CSM McBride, and right now I aint a happy man," the CSM began, "I hear that you men are known as 'fair dinkums' because you joined even after what *me* and all *these* men went through at Gallipoli last year".

An almost arrogant groan echoed through the ranks.

"I wouldn't be feeling too smug if I were you," responded the CSM, "I hear you've been making a nuisance of yourself around Cairo, as well as just acting the larrikin in general".

A few chuckles came from the new men.

"DO YOU BLOKES THINK THIS IS FUNNY?!" Clancy barked in annoyance.

There was not a sound.

"WELL *I* BLOODY DON'T!" shouted Clancy, as he glanced over to the old hands, "and it stops now! The reason that you are here is so that *these* blokes here can teach *you* to be *real* soldiers; and you never know, they *may* even save your life one day".

"Looking at these bampots sir, maybe we won't!" announced Sergeant Mac.

Murmurs of agreement reverberated through the original battalion men.

"Any questions?" asked the CSM, to total silence, "right then, let's start as we mean to go on, become *one* unit, and kick the enemy's arse. PARADE...TO YOUR DUTIES...FALL OUT!"

The Battalion and Brigade staff were obviously thinking on the same lines, as all of the new draft NCOs were reduced to the rank of Private, but were soon re-instated once they had proved themselves to be efficient and competent soldiers; and a vacancy arose.

Following a five week stint at Gebel Habeita, on the 8th of March, the 9th Battalion was relieved by the Light Horse, and set out for Serapeum. There were no signs of the 2nd Light Horse Regiment or a chance of a reunion with Percy and the boys. The move took a while to get under way due to a lack of experience in loading equipment on to camels. No sooner would the laden animal rise to its feet, the harnesses would give way, causing the stricken beasts to topple over on to their sides, where they would lie, kicking about in the dust and screaming and bellowing like spoiled children.

Once on the move, the journey was not an easy one with the terrain alternating between soft sand and hard gravel; not easy on the feet of the men.

"Bloody hell Clance, this isn't good," said Roo, "I'm buggered and my feet are blistered to hell".

"Mine too, but don't show it to these new blokes eh? Got to put up a good show; even though it isn't true," replied a wise Clancy.

As the battalion reached their destination their spirits were raised by the appearance of the band of the 31st Battalion, who had come out specially to meet them. Some of the boys, who had just been dragging along, cheered as the band played marching tunes, and proudly braced up as they marched in to camp at 1900 hours.

Freddy was pleased as the troops marched proudly passed.

"Look at the swagger in the men Clancy. I think things are looking up," uttered the officer.

"Yeah mate. I reckon they'll do eh?" replied Clancy.

At Serapeum training recommenced in earnest and soon it was hard to tell the veterans from the fair dinkums. The new Mark IV Lee Enfield Rifle was issued to all, as well as the Mark VII ammunition, a sharp nosed bullet which replaced the older round nosed version. This lighter nose shifted the centre of gravity of the bullet towards the rear, making it tail heavy. It was also stable in flight and behaved very differently upon hitting the target, inflicting a more severe wound than its predecessor.

"Get hit by this bastard and you won't get up," Clancy noted.

As well as training, there were ample opportunities for a dip in the Suez Canal, a luxury to some, especially with the absence of enemy artillery and sniper fire trying to put an end to their fun.

On the 10th of March the entire 2nd Light Horse Regiment regrouped and moved, via Roda, Deirut and Manfalut, to Assiut, a sizeable town situated beside the Nile. 'C' Squadron remained at Assiut, whilst the rest of the regiment carried on to Sohag, an important centre of administration.

Being sandwiched between two mountain ranges of about two thousand feet in height, the city of Assiut's lower elevation resulted in harsh and chilly, cold winter weather, and a very hot but dry summer.

"It's hot enough to boil a dingo's bum here!" exclaimed Chugger, as he wiped the sweat from his brow with his slouch hat.

During the regimental screening patrols they encountered no enemy, but their show of confidence and strength *did* act as a warning to any hostiles in the Nile area. Alternately they were also a boost to any friendly Arabs, as well as giving the regiment ample opportunity to revise their own skills whilst training the newly arrived re-enforcements in mounted work.

As the new recruits were soon to discover, in their on the job training, lighthorsemen mostly fought dismounted. They were considered to be 'mounted infantry' instead of 'cavalry,' so the soldiers rode horses *to* a battlefield, but they engaged the enemy on foot, leaving quickly on horseback when disengaging. The use of horses made the force more mobile and faster than infantry units and horse-drawn artillery.

During combat, they rode in sections of four lighthorsemen. On contact with the enemy, one soldier would take charge of, and hold the reins, of all four horses, whilst the other three men in his section dismounted and went forward to fight on foot. It was a good system and was working very well.

3

There is no place to hide and so we are found

The 19th of March saw two historical events, the first being a church parade for the 9th and other battalions, with General Birdwood and Edward, Prince of Wales in attendance. The ANZACs could not help but stare at their future King, royal visits to Australia being a rare occurrence, and the chance of a glimpse being reserved usually for city folks. He was rather slight in build, but had a very healthy appearance and looked pleased with the torrent of cheers received from the ANZACs.

The Prince even provided a little entertainment, having tripped and fallen over backwards in full view of the ANZACs, who managed some sly laughter at his mishap. The Prince, embarrassed at his public fall was soon assured of the love and respect of the antipodean soldiers when they spontaneously cheered as he later rode through the camp, lined with loyal and appreciative ANZACs.

The second piece of history was a rumour of an infantry deployment to France, becoming fact; confirmed by General Birdwood no less. The men of the 9th Battalion were ecstatic as this was what they had enlisted for; to give the Hun a good flogging.

There was much to do, including packing up the camp and all equipment. There was a mad rush too by each man to get a letter off to their families to inform them that they were on the move again. But, because of the censor, they could not divulge their destination, so some simply wrote "we're off to somewhere else" or "to the place we originally intended to visit".

The CSM roamed around the camp hurrying the men on.

"Come on fellas you've got about half an hour to get your letters in, so snap to it".

Archie and Roo were very disappointed that they hadn't got to see Percy, but that was the Army, so they quickly scribbled a few lines to him, and wished him well.

At 2000 hours on the 26th of March, after a rousing speech by the CO, and a prayer by the Padre, the battalion entrained to Alexandria. It was a long and freezing night in the crowded and open carriages.

"I think I know what it feels like to be bully beef locked in a tin now," Stowie remarked.

On arrival at the port, the battalion were met by their transport, a Cunard liner, the 'Saxonia', which looked an imposing sight with its long, black hull, a low, well-balanced superstructure, four masts and a single funnel, which was one hundred and six feet tall. They embarked at dawn, followed by the 10th Battalion at 0800 hours, then by eight hundred new arrivals from re-enforcement camps all around Cairo.

"What a rabble those fellows are," said Captain Ponsonby.

Clancy nodded in agreement.

"I hope we don't get any of them. We've only just civilised the other mob".

The 'Saxonia' had a large cargo capacity, but her passenger accommodations were smaller than expected for a liner of her size. As Roo, Archie and Stowie surveyed their new ship, *they* were a little impressed, for bunks had been set up for the other ranks, a far cry from the hammocks on the long journey from Australia. There were even dining halls with proper tables and chairs, with service carried out by the ship's stewards.

"Hey, this is pretty swanky boys, what do you reckon?" asked an impressed Stowie.

"Sure beats the 'Omrah' on the way out," noted Roo.

The accommodation may have been acceptable, but the troops soon discovered that the rations were very small, earning the ship the nickname of the 'Starvonia'.

The 'Saxonia' along with many other troop and hospital ships, finally departed the following day at 0800 hours, escorted by two destroyers and a cruiser. Due to the threat from marauding German submarines, all ranks had to wear life belts, and a watch was established to keep an eye out. The 9th took the first watch, with eager volunteers putting their hands up to sit in the cool breezes on the open deck rather than in the stifling belly of the ship.

Taff and Stowie took the first watch at the stern of the ship, ably assisted by Roo and Archie.

"This has got to be the most popular duty ever eh?" said Archie.

"Aye boyo," replied Taff as he surveyed the packed deck, "they might as well have asked who *doesn't* want to do the duty".

At around 0700 hours on the 31st of March, the 'Saxonia' dropped anchor approximately half a mile off the coast of Malta. All on board admired the rocky coastline from their vantage points on the ship, as they did the following day as the ship cruised past the islands of Sardinia and Corsica.

Archie, a lover of history was quick to point out that Napoleon had been born on Corsica.

"He was a great general you know, and the French were the masters of mainland Europe," he announced excitedly.

"Well they aint the masters anymore are they?" replied Clancy.

On the 2nd of April France finally came in to view, it's warm and sunny Mediterranean coastline lulling the ANZAC soldiers in to a false sense of security.

"This doesn't look too bad boys," said Clancy.

"Ah...but this *is* the warm bit old chap," answered Ponsonby, "where we're going has a tendency to be a little cold and somewhat damp".

"Bloody great! There's always someone to put a dampener on things," Clancy replied.

As the 'Saxonia' slipped in to Marseilles Harbour, it sailed closely past two hospital ships full of British soldiers lying on stretchers out on the deck. On seeing this, the mood for some of the ANZACs turned gloomy until Clancy suddenly began to cheer vociferously for the Tommies. This cheering soon caused a ripple effect, creating a tidal wave of cheerful shouts and applause in the direction of the wounded men, some of whom becoming suddenly animated, waving back to their antipodean allies.

The battalion disembarked at around 0745 hours and each man was issued rations enough for fifty eight hours. On the wharf were many German prisoners of war, guarded by elderly looking French soldiers dressed in sky blue tunics, red trousers and a cap. They had been allotted this duty in order to free up younger soldiers for the front line.

The German prisoners, in their field grey uniforms, appeared defiant as they briefly paused from their work in order to admire their new foe.

"G'day Fritz," said Stowie, "we've come to kick your imperial asses".

Some of the Germans could obviously understand English as one stepped towards Stowie, but was quickly prodded back in to place with a bayonet from one of the French guards.

"You'll keep mate," Clancy added.

As the soldiers marched along the worn wooden planks of

Marseille's harbour, they were met with a scene straight from history, the old port unfolding before them. The harbour, dating back to ancient Greek settlers in 600BC, had been the heart of Marseille since its inception, and as the men gazed in awe at the ancient stone buildings and the boats swaying gently in the harbour, they momentarily forgot why they were there, and that they were at war.

Marching over the cobblestone roads towards the railway station, the ANZACs were very quickly initiated into French culture, as crowds of locals lined the mediaeval streets shouting a welcome to the men whose reputation had quite obviously preceded them.

"BIENVENUE LES AUSTRALIANS" came the shouts from the gathered crowd.

But there was more than that, as eager women began throwing their arms around individual soldiers and kissing their cheeks.

Clancy was particularly happy about the female attention.

"I could do this every day," he called out to Ponsonby, "viv la France".

But pretty soon the men received rather a large culture shock, with burly and sweaty French men grasping hold of their faces and planting sloppy and unwelcome kisses on unsuspecting cheeks.

"What the blazes?!" exclaimed Roo as he pushed away a swooning Frenchman.

"It's just their way Roo, dear chap. They are *very* grateful," said Captain Ponsonby.

"There's grateful, and there's...well, you know...grateful," growled Clancy as he took a swipe at an overzealous citizen and then held up his tightly clenched fist, "kiss me again mate and you'll be wearing this!"

Despite the language barrier the French man got the message and turned his attention to another Aussie soldier.

The troops were relieved, to say the least, to finally begin boarding their troop train, which consisted of wooden passenger carriages with both doors and windows; a far cry from the open trucks in Egypt.

Archie took one look at the carriages and turned to Clancy.

"Do you think they have first and second class on here mate?"

Clancy laughed

"I'm the CSM now mate so if there *is* first class then I'll be on the posh ones with the officers, isn't that right Freddy?"

"It certainly is old boy. RHIP and all that," replied Freddy, "but alas, it is the same class for all".

"RHIP?" asked Stowie.

"Rank has its privileges," replied Freddy.

"Well, if there's no first class then I'll be buggered if I sit with you load of toffs when I can be with my mates here," said Clancy.

"Suit yourself sergeant major. Cocktails anyone?" replied Captain Ponsonby with a cheeky wink.

Their journey would take them from Marseilles, through towns such as Lyon, Dijon, and Versailles, on to their final, as yet unknown, destination. The journey from south to north was almost through the whole length of the country, and took them towards the region of the Belgian border. To all who surveyed the sprawling countryside, France appeared to be a beautiful country, its green and productive areas untouched by war. It was spring, and all vegetation was bursting out in blossoms and green foliage; a stark contrast to the barren deserts of Egypt. The men admired the many sights and steep sided valleys through which the railway had been cut, as well as the stone bridges, walls and the green hedgerows which had stood for centuries, and no doubt could tell a story or two about past conflicts which had occurred in this land. However, the Aussies noticed, in the fields, the absence of young men, who were most likely away at the front, or dead. They also observed that many of the women that they saw appeared to be dressed in black, which gave the impression that France must be in mourning.

The battalion had now bonded from its mixture of raw and veteran soldiers, their troublesome tendencies being cast out of them by the discipline and training dished out by the Warrant Officers and NCOs.

As the train ambled through the lush countryside to its unknown destination, it paused occasionally at villages for coal and water re-supply, thus giving the troops an opportunity to alight from the carriages and breathe in the fresh air, even for just a few minutes. On their journey, and at the various stops, they encountered cheery French townsfolk, eager to acquire badges and buttons as souvenirs. Some enterprising locals even sold baguettes and fresh fruit to the ANZACs...at fair prices.

"These Frenchies are fairer and better mannered than the gyppos eh?" said Taff.

"Yes, makes a nice change doesn't it?" replied Roo.

"And they don't rip you off either," added Archie, as he tucked in to his baguette.

At one point the locomotive braked suddenly, causing each carriage, none of which had brakes, to clickety clack and crash in to one another, thus coming to a ricocheting and jolting halt.

Clancy, who was hanging out of the window at the time, banged his head against the frame.

"Bugger!" he exclaimed, whilst rubbing his head.

Roo was now on his feet and at the window.

"Hey, look at that," he said, having spotted a stream a few yards from the track, "are you thinking what I'm thinking?"

It appeared that the majority of the battalion were having similar thoughts as they sprang from their carriages and raced towards the stream, for a quick wash. A couple of days in a stuffy carriage was doing no-one's noses any favours.

"Bloody luxury!" Clancy exclaimed as he unbuttoned his tunic and shirt and began splashing the cool stream water on his face and under his arm pits.

"Too right mate. It's a big difference from the desert eh?" Roo responded.

The men relished their wash, and the break from the cramped and stuffy conditions on the train, but their enjoyment, and momentary lapse, from the worry of their re-engagement with the Great War, was soon cut short, a loud and sudden piercing shriek from the waiting locomotive causing all heads to turn simultaneously in a manoeuvre worthy of an eyes right on the parade ground.

"That's it. Fun's over boys," shouted Archie, "back to the train".

As the soldiers began making their way up the gentle slope,

the engine driver had ideas of his own, as the train hissed and jolted forward.

"Hey, you bastard! Wait for us!" Clancy called out.

"RUN!" came a voice from the now clean soldiers.

A dawdle turned into a mad dash for the train, with most seeing the funny side as they sprinted, giggling like a bunch of school girls.

Many hands reached out from the carriages to haul their mates on board.

Clancy was the last man back on the train, having made a quick visual sweep of the area to ensure that no man had been left behind.

"That was lucky boys," he uttered, feeling relieved, but refreshed, at the same time.

The men quickly became accustomed to the unpredictability of the troop trains, and not knowing when, or how long it would be, until their next stop, often having to resort to taking toilet breaks directly out of the doors of the moving locomotive; much to the occasional surprise of passing locals.

Late in the morning of the 5th of April, after two and a half days travelling, the train rolled in to the village of Godewaersvelde, situated a few miles from Ypres.

"I'll be glad to get off. My backside is bloody sore from sitting down all the time," announced Clancy as he peered out at the station sign, "hey Taff, I think we're in *your* country mate, have you seen the name of this place on the sign?"

As Taff stuck his head out of the window he was astonished.

"My goodness boyo I think you could be right...

God...ewaers...velde. I don't even think *I* can pronounce that one".

"These place names are going to be hard to get used to. Give me a good old Aussie name like Cunnamulla or Goondiwindi any day," laughed Clancy, as he thought to himself about a new version of the name of this particular town.

"I know, let's make it simple and call if Gerty Wears Velvet," he announced, to approving nods and smiles.

As the train ground to a halt, Clancy shouted to the SNCOs to get the men formed up into their various companies. He, accompanied by the RSM and other CSMs, then strode out to locate the officers.

As Clancy approached his OC, who was stood with a young lieutenant, he was greeted warmly.

"Clancy old chap. Good trip was it?" asked Captain Ponsonby.

"Freddy mate, it was pretty good. The smell got a bit ripe towards the end, but we stank worse at Gallipoli eh?" replied the CSM, "anyhow, what's happening now?"

"We're going to be billeted at some farms in the villages of Strazeele, Merris and Meteren," said Ponsonby, "they're about five miles away, so get the men ready for a march; you know, plenty of water and all that?"

The lieutenant, noticing that Clancy had not saluted either himself or the captain, felt agitated and was quick to challenge the CSM.

"Don't you salute officers, sergeant major?" he growled.

Clancy made a cursory glance at the lieutenant.

"Who's this boy Freddy?"

"I asked *you* a question," demanded the lieutenant.

"Yes I do...sir...but not in a war zone...unless you want your head blown off by enemy snipers," the CSM growled back, "would you *like* me to salute you mate?"

The officer was taken aback by the forthright manner of the CSM, and when Clancy started to move his right arm, he quickly jumped in.

"NO! No I don't."

"Good decision son," Clancy retorted.

An awkward silence followed, until it was broken by Captain Ponsonby.

"CSM, this is Lieutenant Thomas Sargent. He is the new commander of Number 5 Platoon.

"Roo and Archie's platoon?" replied Clancy, giving the lieutenant a scornful glance.

"Yes. So if you can get him settled in it would be appreciated. We move in thirty minutes," said the Captain.

As Captain Ponsonby walked away, Clancy and Lieutenant Sargent stood together, an awkward silence blanketing the two men.

It was Clancy who broke it.

"Sargent? That's a good name for a soldier," said Clancy, feeling quite uncomfortable in the officer's presence.

"It would be even more uncomfortable if you were *actually* a Sergeant. Perhaps that's why I became an officer" replied the lieutenant.

"Sergeant Sargent eh? Yeah, I see what you mean," replied Clancy, "but no fear of that for you eh?"

The company needed to form up before their move and time was ticking away.

"Righto, come on Mr Sargent," said Clancy.

As they walked the atmosphere calmed and the two men began to chat.

"What's my platoon like?" asked Lieutenant Sargent.

"Good blokes. Most are Gallipoli veterans and the rest are fair dinks, but they've blended in well. Your SNCOs are good men".

Clancy pondered for a moment.

"A bit of advice?" he asked.

"Go on," replied the officer.

"Get off your high horse and learn from these men," replied Clancy, as he recalled similar advice given to a new officer at Gallipoli, by Ponsonby.

Lieutenant Sargent stopped in his tracks, the CSM following suit.

"Well, that was right to the point CSM," replied the young officer, feeling less tense, "but, in a way, I was hoping you would say that. I don't know what I'm doing and really *do* need your help".

Clancy's respect for Sargent was beginning to increase, as he appreciated honesty and an admission that someone did not know everything. What he didn't want in a brand new officer was some "jumped up know it all" who would get his mates killed.

"Listen, sir, none of us knew about war, and sort of learned on the job so to speak," Clancy responded, "you've got two good sergeants in Roo and Archie, so get to know them, and learn from them…oh, and it's Clancy when it's just us".

Lieutenant Sargent held out a hand of friendship and gratitude to Clancy.

"Thank you Clancy. I think we'll get on well," replied the much relieved Lieutenant, "and my name is Thomas...and, sorry about before".

Clancy smiled and shook the Lieutenant's hand vigorously.

"Good to meet you Tomo".

The battalion was soon on the march again, singing as they went, with songs like 'Waltzing Matilda' sung in an almost defiant manner, warning the Germans that the Australians had arrived. Some even made songs up as they went.

"Onward, Christian soldiers, marching on to war, with a lot of corporals who have never seen war before".

After this particular one Stowie joked "hey you fellas, us corporals have got feelings you know".

The scenery was quite picturesque, with a smooth, slowly rising landscape and fertile valleys, but the distant artillery fire was a reminder to the men of what awaited them ahead.

Lieutenant Sargent was feeling nervous already as he flinched at each sound of exploding artillery shells. Clancy, who didn't miss a trick, gently grasped the officer's shoulder.

"There's nothing wrong with being scared Tomo, but you need to hide your fears from these blokes. Me and you can't *afford* to show fear, because *we* are what the troops need to focus *their* courage on," Clancy wisely advised.

"Thanks Clance," replied Tomo, who, composing himself, quickly turned to the marching soldiers, "when you've finished insulting the corporals, you blokes *must* have a song or two about officers".

A trickle of laughter went through the ranks, the men appreciative of Tomo's candour.

"Too right we have mate," a voice answered, as the men spontaneously broke into a chorus of "one staff officer jumped right over another staff officer's back..."

"Good on yer sir," said Clancy, patting the officer on his back, "you'll do for me".

The billets were a far cry from the dugouts on the peninsula and the tents of Egypt, and consisted of courtyards surrounded by farm houses, barns and stables. Within the courtyards were deep pits which were used for the dumping of household waste and manure. Each farm was surrounded by a high wall, left over from past centuries when even a Frenchman's home *was* his castle, designed to keep out those who sought to harm or steal from them.

"Sergeant Major McBride," Captain Ponsonby called out.

"Sir!" replied Clancy.

"The barns and stables have been allocated to the SNCOs and other ranks. The officers will be in the farm house," said Ponsonby.

"Oh yeah...alright for some eh?" Clancy joked.

"Got to keep up appearances old boy," laughed Ponsonby.

At this point, Roo and Archie had joined the group.

"I don't suppose I can bunk with you chaps?" asked Tomo, "you know, just to get to know you a bit better".

"I don't know about that mate," replied Roo.

"Why is that?" enquired Tomo, feeling a little disappointed.

Roo looked at Archie and smiled.

"It's the only time and place us and the boys have to talk about you," he replied.

"*Really?*" asked a surprised Tomo.

Clancy gave Tomo a friendly punch on the arm.

"It's only good stuff though, eh fellas?" he joked.

Archie coughed.

"Yeah...right," he replied.

Captain Ponsonby quickly retrieved the situation.

"Come on Tommy, let's go to our warm and comfortable farmhouse and talk about this rabble," he said, winking slyly at Clancy, Archie and Roo.

The next two weeks was a very wet period, which made a nice change for the battalion after the Middle Eastern heat, with some even jumping out in the rain, with a bar of soap, for an impromptu shower. There was also much training in order to "acclimatise" to the new terrain and type of warfare, including route marches along the many cobbled roads. After becoming accustomed to soft sand over the past few months, these harder surfaces played havoc not only with their Aussie boots, but also with blisters. Although of good quality, their boots had been bleached and dried by the desert sun and now fell apart with the wet European weather. Foot inspections became the norm, and revealed to Clancy that a few were not washing or changing their socks as often as they should.

"Bloody hell boys those socks stink of cheese; and some of them can probably stand up and walk around by themselves!"

After receiving replacement general pattern boots, a new stout Australian boot was eventually issued and was a good fit with the weather and conditions. All in all though, it had been an uncomfortable period for the 9th.

With this new type of warfare came many new weapons. Gas was being used quite frequently, much to the disgust of the men.

"What sort of bloody war *is* this, trying to poison a fella?" growled Taff.

Stowie rolled his eyes and replied sarcastically.

"Yeah, I'd rather be machine gunned and bombed any day".

"Eh?" asked a surprised Taff, then it dawned on what Stowie had just said, "oh yes, I see what you mean boyo".

This particular day had been earmarked as a gas training day.

Each man had been issued a PH Helmet, which was made up of a flannel bag, with transparent eye pieces. It was a crude piece of equipment, which fitted over the head, the open end being tucked in to the wearer's tunic. The mask was soaked in a liquid which supposedly killed any gas fumes, and the wearer would breathe out through a metal tube which was held in their mouth.

Clancy was in charge of the training, teaching the company platoon by platoon. The men formed up in front of a long trench which was full of a fog that hung at low level in the trench.

"Right you blokes, this is a trench full of gas...not the killer stuff," announced the CSM, "on the battlefield we need to inform everyone if there is gas present. We do this with a trench rattle...like so...or banging something metal together and shouting gas! gas! gas! However, before you do this, you need to save yourself. Pay attention while I demonstrate".

At that, Clancy closed his eyes, stopped breathing and turned his back to the wind, leaned forward, donned his respirator, blew out, and shouted:

"GAS! GAS! GAS!"

"And you need to do that as fast as lightning boys. Nine seconds will do the trick I think," Clancy said, his voice muffled by the mask.

"Sorry, can you say that again CSM?" joked Stowie, resulting in spontaneous laughter from the platoon.

Clancy glared at the men to his front.

"Perhaps you can all hear *this*...GAS! GAS! GAS!" he shouted, catching the men off guard, "come on you bludgers, mask up NOW! NINE...EIGHT...SEVEN...bloody hurry up or you'll all be dead!"

The men fumbled for their masks and carried out the manoeuvre as instructed.

"ONE...ZERO!" shouted Clancy, feeling satisfied as he scanned all present, each now resembling locusts, in their PH Helmets, "what a handsome bunch you all look...CORPORAL STOWE!"

"Yes sir?" replied Stowie.

"You're a bit of a funny bloke. In to that trench and walk to the end," instructed Clancy.

"What, through that stuff?" replied Stowie.

"Yep," said Clancy, looking impatient, "not so funny now is it...well?"

Stowie shrugged his shoulders and jumped down into the gas filled trench, disappearing out of sight. Everyone present looked on with baited breath, waiting for him to resurface. Sure enough, Stowie's head and arms appeared on the 'surface' as he began to feign swimming along the trench. Once at the other end he calmly climbed out and bowed to his audience.

"That wasn't too bad boys; in you get," said Stowie as he beckoned the rest of the platoon to take their turn.

Still wearing his mask, Clancy stood, hands on hips, shaking his head, but smiling a concealed smile.

"You cheeky bugger Stowie," he said, then, turning to the platoon, shouted, "COME ON THEN, WHAT ARE YOU WAITING FOR?"

The men took to the training very easily and pretty soon all had completed their 'swim'.

Once the last man had clambered out of the trench, Clancy removed his mask, inhaled some fresh air, and ordered the men to do the same.

"Good work boys," he said proudly.

In truth, each man was relieved to remove the cumbersome device from their heads as the masks were damp and sticky, as well as uncomfortable and stuffy.

"Let's hope we never have to use these bloody things for real," Archie whispered to Roo.

"Bloody oath," replied his cousin.

4

Easy does it

Unlike their dramatic landing at Gallipoli, the ANZACs, on arrival in France, were placed in a nursery section just south of Armentieres, in order to get them accustomed to this new theatre of war.

As the battalion marched to their destination they were reminded of a song which was set in this part of France.

"Come on lads, let's hear you sing it then," shouted the CSM, "I know you're all itching to".

But there was silence.

"Hey Taff!" said Clancy.

"Yes mate?" replied Taff.

"You Welsh blokes love your singing don't you?" said Clancy, with a wink and a nod.

"Oh, all right then," said Taff, "I'll get the boys started then shall I?"

Taff cleared his throat, did a quick hum, and began.

"*Mademoiselle from Armentieres, parle vous, hadn't been kissed for forty years, parle vous. She surrendered every night, didn't even put up a fight, rinky dinky parle vous*".

The song soon flowed throughout the battalion, and worried expressions turned to smiles, as the men felt a new vigour, bracing up and setting a fast marching pace.

"That's it lads," shouted a proud Captain Ponsonby, "get some swagger into you!"

The battalion spent the next eight days practising scouting, trench raids, gas attacks and warnings, before moving out to Sailly-Sur-La-Lys, about five miles to the west.

As they marched, for some of the uninitiated troops it seemed the most exciting march imaginable, with guns all around them crashing and roaring until sometimes it was impossible to hear one another speak. But all was about to change.

Within hours the 9th Battalion was in the trenches of France, having relieved the 17th Lancashire Fusiliers. Rue Du Bois was a long road running from north east to south east, and was the firing line. 'A' Company was placed in close support, whilst the remaining companies were in support to their rear.

Apart from intermittent small arms and machine gun fire, all was quiet; but for those in the rear trench there was work to be done.

The experienced men had immediately noticed that the existing defensive rampart was very low and not only useless, but dangerous to the tall Aussies.

"These poms are a bunch of short arses skipper," said Clancy.

"Steady on…I *could* be offended by that remark," replied Ponsonby.

"And *are* you?" asked the CSM.

"Of course not, but our *heads* will *definitely* be if the old Hun notices, so we'd better get the height increased quick smart eh?" advised Ponsonby.

"No worries mate," replied the CSM.

Work quickly commenced and, in no time, the parapet was a safer height, neatly sandbagged and fitted with periscopes.

The men were impressed with their work and were soon relaxing, talking of home, and wondering what the next few hours and days had in store for them.

"When are we going to get to have a crack at the Germans?" asked an impatient Private Kropp.

"I wouldn't be any rush mate," said Roo.

"Well, I'm not scared. I was top at everything in training you know," replied Kropp.

"Really?" replied Archie, "bully for you. It's a different story when you meet the enemy face to face. *Everyone* is scared".

"Not me," said Kropp.

Clancy was not happy.

"Mate, you'll shit yourself the first time some bastard shoots at you!"

"No way mate...er...sir. The Germans don't scare me," replied Private Kropp.

As Clancy turned his back on the arrogant soldier he beckoned Roo and Archie to walk with him, whispering to each other as they strolled.

Tuesday the 25th of April 1916 was the very first ANZAC Day and commemorations took place with an inspection by Generals Plumer, Wallis, White, and the Brigadier, with each battalion being addressed later by Plumer and MacLagan; followed by company sports.

A few days later they had a visit from, no less than, Field Marshall Haig, the Commander in Chief of British Armies in France.

"Do you think we should do the book binder thing again if spoken to?" asked Taff.

Clancy laughed.

"Not this time mate. He'll probably have you shot!"

The sector was so quiet that French civilians still occupied their homes as far forward as the support lines and the trenches.

The 29th of April was just another spring day and, although the days were getting longer, the nights were still bitterly cold.

"Good job we bought some new sleeping bags in Cairo eh Roo?" said Archie.

There was no response from Roo. He just stared forward, his eyes locked on the ground to his front.

Clancy nudged Archie.

"What's up with Roo? He looks like he's dropped sixpence and found a penny," said Clancy, "hey Roo mate, why are you looking so glum?"

Roo suddenly awoke from his trance.

"Eh?" he asked, rubbing his eyes.

"Why are you so glum mate?" Clancy asked again.

"Oh, just a feeling," Roo replied.

"What feeling?" asked Archie.

"Like something bad is about to happen," replied Roo.

"Like something bad is about to happen?!" exclaimed Clancy, "Of course it is mate, we're in a war".

"Yeah, but I forgot to make peace with the ancestors and spirits when we first arrived, with all the rush and hullabaloo," said Roo, a concerned expression covering his face.

"Bugger," said Clancy, "that served us well at Gallipoli. Is it too late to do it now?"

"I don't know, but we could give it a lash," replied Roo.

Roo glanced towards each of his mates.

"First you all need to pick up a small rock from the ground and hold it in your hand for a moment" said Roo.

The men looked at each other briefly, and then each soldier bent down and scooped up a small pebble as instructed. Roo also picked up a handful of dust, licked his fingers then dipped them in to the dirt.

"What's he doing Archie?" asked Kropp.

"Ssshhhh, let Roo carry on," whispered Archie to the inquisitive young soldier.

Next Roo unbuttoned his tunic and began to smear the wet

soil on to his forehead, across his chest and on the palms of his hands. This signalled to the spirits that they were ready to receive blessings or wise words. He then raised his head and eyes upward and began to speak.

"Spirits, of all of our ancestors, above, I thank you for all of my new family here present, and for making us part of the sky, nature and the land which owns us. I ask that you welcome these good people here to this land, keep them safe from harm, keep their resolve steady, and return them safely home when all of this is over".

Roo then spoke to his mates directly.

"Right, you each need to toss your stone in to the air and ask the spirits to welcome you. Here, let me show you," said Roo as he tossed his pebble upwards, "I am Rueben Taylor, I am in *your* country; please welcome me."

There was a group murmur, and a hurling, and thudding, of rocks as they hit the ground and the sandbagged parapet in quick succession, with each man uttering the words as instructed.

Roo was content.

"Is that it?" asked Private Kropp.

Clancy was becoming very frustrated at the rudeness of young Kropp and was just about to show him his fist when Captain Ponsonby and Lieutenant Sargent, who had been doing the rounds of the company, arrived.

Roo, upon seeing what was about to occur, tapped Clancy on the shoulder and whispered.

"He'll keep mate".

"Evening men," said a jovial Ponsonby, "I've got some good news; we're sleeping in a barn tonight".

"Hallelujah!" whispered Stowie.

"Yes, we're coming off the line for a few days, down the road to Rouge de Bout," added Ponsonby, "and bunking down with 'C' Company".

Once at the farm, Roo was still feeling and looking worried. As he scanned the many huts, barns and other buildings, he felt a sense of impending doom.

"Fellas, I'm sleeping under the stars tonight," he announced.

"Really? Its brass monkey weather mate!" exclaimed a surprised Clancy.

"Something just doesn't seem right boys," replied Roo.

Clancy pondered to himself.

"Well, I'm kipping alongside you then mate," announced Clancy.

Not to be left out, Archie, Taff and Stowie joined them.

The five men shivered their way through a cold night, but awoke refreshed, despite being soaked through by the morning dew.

"Bugger!" uttered Clancy.

"Well, we may be wet, but we're still here boys," added Stowie.

Clancy glanced over to Roo.

"How are you feeling today mate?" he asked.

"I dunno. Still a bit strange," replied Roo.

The company's day of rest was just that, for a change, with many choosing to remain in the relative warmth of their accommodation.

Clancy, however, had other ideas, and soon rounded up enough men for a friendly game of cricket, 'B' Company versus

'C' Company, also managing to entice enough of the troops outside to act as the crowd.

The French sun was warm, amidst the rolling fields near the front lines, and the Australian troops found a temporary respite from the thoughts of war that constantly filled their heads. The makeshift pitch, marked by two empty wooden crates as wickets, saw soldiers from both companies eagerly displaying their cricketing prowess.

Captain Ponsonby, a former public school cricketer, was selected as 'B' Company's bowler, and delivered a well aimed ball down the pitch, causing 'C' Company's batsman to swing his bat with determination. The crack of wood meeting leather echoed across the field as the ball soared into the air. Cheers erupted from both sides as fielders, and spectators, scrambled to catch it, their shouts mingling with the distant rumble of artillery.

As the game went on, the competition heated up, but so did the sense of unity among the players. Despite the rivalry, there were moments of camaraderie as spectators from opposing sides shared a drink or swapped stories during breaks.

At around 1315 hours, however, Roo's worries became real when there was a sudden distant rumble which grew louder, all heads turning skyward as approximately sixty high explosive shells, from enemy 5.9 inch Howitzers, came screaming through the air, raining down on 'C' Company's billets.

The jovial atmosphere shattered like glass as the ground shook with each subsequent explosion; dust and debris billowing up from the impact site. There were cries of "Take cover!" as the cricketers and spectators instinctively scattered to form a hodge podge defensive line, just in case this was the prelude to a German attack.

But none came.

As Ponsonby stood and brushed himself off he surveyed the immediate area.

"Perhaps the Huns just don't appreciate cricket," he joked

"Just like me," added Stowie.

But, as the dust settled and the acrid scent of smoke lingered in the air, the full extent of the damage became painfully apparent.

One round had scored a direct hit on a hut, wounding four of the occupants, whilst another shell had wounded others who were running to their aid. Another large group of soldiers had been sheltering behind a brick building when a shell struck the wall, killing twenty five and wounding another forty seven. Among the soldiers, who had sought shelter, there were grim scenes of tragedy. Some lay motionless, their bodies battered and broken by the force of the explosions, whilst others groaned in agony, their faces contorted with pain as they clutched at wounds inflicted by flying shrapnel. Mates rushed to their aid, doing their best with what little they had to bandage gaping wounds.

The 9th Battalion had arrived in France with nine hundred and sixty men and already they had lost a third of a company.

On Good Friday 1916 a further enemy bombardment, which this time landed in an empty field, sealed the deal, with the battalion marching out to Sailly. It appeared that even the so called safe areas were not actually safe.

"You were right mate," said Clancy to Roo.

"Sadly, I was".

Although hygiene standards were higher than on the peninsula, things and facilities still could have been better.

"The colonel has a gift for you boys," announced Captain Ponsonby.

"A gift?" asked Clancy.

"Yes. Fall the company in, we're off for a bit of a stroll sergeant major," replied Ponsonby, feeling rather smug.

"Perhaps we're off to a knocking shop," said one soldier.

"If we are then they can count me out," said Roo.

"Me too," said Taff, "I don't want a dose of the clap".

"...again!" a voice echoed from the ranks, followed by much laughter.

Taff looked around the files of men.

"I recognised that voice, you cheeky sod...you'll get yours boyo!" he growled, "and just because your name sounds Welsh, don't think you'll get away with it".

The owner of the voice was one Private John Leak, originally from Portsmouth in England, but now an Aussie soldier. He was the son of a miner, with parents who had emigrated from South Wales to Australia years earlier. By the outbreak of the war, both his parents had passed away, and Leak was living in Clermont, Queensland, working as a teamster. On the 28th of January 1915, he had enlisted at Rockhampton and was assigned to the fifth reinforcement draft for the 9th Battalion, arriving at ANZAC Cove on the 22nd of June.

As the battalion reached the village, their gift, a pleasant surprise for the battalion, was laid out before them...a bath house.

"Look at that boys; there's a bath tub for each of us," said an excited Private Leak.

"Showers too," added Roo.

The men thoroughly enjoyed their hot baths, but the showers not so much, for, in order not to waste the valuable hot water, they were only turned on for a few minutes, often shutting down, leaving the user still caked in soap.

The men's under garments were taken off them and replaced with a fresh, clean, issue.

"Crikey Arch, your undies looked like they were coming alive!" laughed Clancy.

"You can talk mate. Yours gave me a hug and shook my hand before they left," replied Archie.

One thing the men were *definitely* appreciative of was the fact that while they were bathing, their uniforms were fumigated. Finally the lessons of trench warfare were sinking in.

By the end of April spring was finally setting in. The weather was noticeably warmer, and the trees were in blossom.

On the 5th of May all ranks were issued with the new steel helmet. It was modelled on the medieval helmet of centuries ago with its basin like appearance and wide brim, and was gratefully received by the troops, for they now had protection from flying debris and shrapnel from above. Clancy was quick to encourage the men to camouflage the helmets with hessian and to add netting on which to tie scraps of material and hessian in order to break up their outline.

By the middle of May 1916 the 9th Battalion was finally posted to a section of the front line, having moved to the Petillon section, two miles south of Fleurbaix. The geography of the landscape was very flat, and consisted of small hamlets, pretty churches and hedge lined lanes, with farmers' fields stretching as far as the eye could see.

"We've certainly got some good fields of fire here Clance," said Roo.

Clancy had a concerned look on his face.

"Yeah, that's what worries me. If *we* have such a good view, then so do the Germans," replied Clancy as he stroked his chin.

Lessons had indeed been learned since 1914. When a company was relieved, all stores, such as ammunition, bombs, periscopes, very lights, maps, and all manner of equipment, remained in the sector, so it was up to the Quartermaster (QM) and the Regimental Quartermaster Sergeant (RQMS) and Company Quartermaster Sergeant (CQMS) and their staff, to ensure that the stores were always full and replenished.

As the English soldiers that they were relieving departed the trench the Aussies weren't impressed. There was much damage to the breastworks from shell fire, and the parapet and defences in general required raising in height, as well as strengthening.

"I don't think these poms care skipper," said Clancy, "this place is a bloody shambles".

"I think they do. Poor leadership is to blame, in my opinion," replied Freddy.

"Well, we've got a lot of work to do, but not until its dark," said Clancy.

"Yeah, don't want to be easy targets for the Huns eh?" added Archie.

A snap orders group was held by the OC, with Platoon Commanders, SNCOs and Section Commanders in attendance. It was decided that the men would occupy the parapets, with every third man grabbing a four hour sleep.

"Two hours on and four hours off should do it, with two thirds of the company manning the line," said Ponsonby, "and the remainder will be sleeping and doing fatigues during the night".

"Sounds like a good plan," said Clancy turning his gaze to the NCOs, "righto, let's get to it fellas".

Due to the flat, swampy nature of the terrain in this sector the front line was not really a trench as such, but a breastwork constructed from sandbags. It was eight feet high and around ten feet thick, with built in fire steps. Quite a sight.

Everything went as planned, with the battalion either keeping watch in the front line trench, on fatigues or resting.

As long as you kept your head down you were comparatively safe. Stowie and his section were on sentry duty for a couple of hours on the first night, from 0100 hours to 0300 hours, and he had instructed his men to keep a sharp look out. The troops did not care for the idea of keeping their heads above the trench and looking for the Germans, however it *had* to be done. It was quite uncanny for the Aussies to watch the enemy trench, which appeared somewhat like a black wave and only a couple of hundred yards in front, especially when they would suddenly see the flash of their rifles and machine guns, followed immediately by the guns' report and nasty thuds on the sandbags which the men were resting against. Stowie fired about five shots at their flashes, the only target to aim at, but another two rounds which lodged in the parapet either side of his head, leaving about two to three inches between him and certain death, soon changed his mind about wasting ammunition in the darkness.

The least popular fatigue duty was the siting and re-supply for the "Imshee Battery", a battery of sixty pounder trench mortars. On one particular night it was the turn of Taff and his section. They soon experienced the clumsy weight of these weapons and their projectiles.

"Flaming heck these things must weigh a ton," complained Private Leak.

"Half a hundred weight to be precise," responded one of the crew members, "and that's just the shell".

Taff, his section, and the crews of the battery moved uneasily, but stealthily, through the sandbagged corridor that was the sap, up to the firing position. As they laid down the mortars and their missiles, the battery crews expertly took over, assembling the mortars with precision, then setting their sights. The battery corporal then gave the thumbs up to each crew, who readied their projectiles.

On the command "Ten rounds HE...hang", the mortar men held their mortar rounds over the mouth of the respective tubes.

The order came, "FIRE!", as the rounds were dropped into their tubes. This was followed by a "pfft" noise as each round flew skywards, arcing in the air, then nose diving awkwardly in to the German trenches. The rounds were slow, and before the first one had reached its target, the second round was already in the air. Taff and his section marvelled at the efficiency of the mortar crews, but, no sooner had they begun their deadly work, all ten rounds per weapon had been expended.

There was no time or point in whispering now, for the Germans would soon be responding with a retaliatory barrage.

"Right boys, dismantle your kit and let's get the hell out of here," shouted the corporal.

In reality the crews did not wait for the order for they knew what was coming.

Taff and the boys snatched up the mortar pieces very quickly, and what was once heavy, now seemed weightless, as the adrenaline fuelled soldiers ran back down the sap to relative safety, as enemy mortar rounds exploded all around showering them with mud and rocks.

Upon reaching the front line trench, the occupants thanked them for the ferocious bombardment that they were now receiving as a result of their fire mission.

"Don't mention it boys," said Taff, as he threw up a smart salute to his unappreciative mates.

During the Easter of 1916, in Egypt, news was received of disastrous attacks by the Turks on the eastern posts at Katia, Duidar and Hammisah, which had been held by the Warwick, Worcester and Gloucester Yeomanry. On the 11th and 13th of May the 2nd Light Horse Regiment entrained from Assiut and Sohag for Kantara. On the 18th of May they crossed the canal to Hill 70 and on the 26th of May they marched to Romani, twenty two miles from the Suez Canal, and about seven miles from the ancient Pelusium, where a major battle had been fought between the Achaemenid Empire of Persia and Pharaohs of Egypt.

The Sinai Campaign was just about to commence.

At the beginning of the campaign most of the regiment's horses had contracted Nile Fever, and they required constant nursing by their riders. This, added to the fact that the climate had taken its toll on the men, did not make for a welcome start to the campaign.

The 2nd Light Horse Regiment relieved the 2nd Brigade at Romani and was soon introduced to tiring desert patrols, which tested the men and their mounts for the months to come.

Following their successful raids on the eastern posts, the Turks had withdrawn across the desert, instead of capitalising on the advantage. This puzzled the men, but they were grateful for the error that the Turkish and German commanders had made.

The Turkish patrols, utilising camels, were encountered at Bir-el-Add, Salmana, and Bay'ud. Their fortified posts of some strength were at Mazar and El-Arish, thirty seven and fifty six miles, respectively, from Romani.

For three days, commencing on the 29th of May, the 2nd Light Horse acted as covering troops to the New Zealand Mounted Rifle Brigade, as they scouted Bir Salmana, some twenty five miles distant. Water was always scarce whilst patrolling, with the well water being foul, resulting in unpleasant tea but tolerable coffee. Even the horses were reluctant to drink it, making *their* health even worse. Travelling over the desert sand in the hot and dry conditions was strenuous, for both man and beast, so for ten minutes every hour the men dismounted and led their horses on foot, thus giving them at least a little respite.

"I can't believe we've been out here for three days already," remarked Chugger as he wiped sweat from his brow, "it feels like we've been crossing this blasted desert forever".

"I know what you mean," replied Davo, "the heat I can take, but the water...ugh...I don't know how much more of that foul tea I can stomach".

"At least the coffee's passable," said Boggy, smiling and raising his eyebrows, "but I feel a bit guilty when even the horses won't drink."

"I bet they miss the lush pastures back home," Davo said, patting his horse's neck, "I sure do. Can't stop thinking about the rolling green hills and the smell of fresh rain on the farm in the summer".

"Yeah, and a decent meal," added Percy, joining the conversation, "mum's Sunday roast...I'd give anything for a taste of that right now".

"Bloody hell Perce you've made my stomach rumble now," laughed Chugger.

The men fell silent for a moment, lost in thoughts of home. The landscape, harsh and unyielding, stretched out before them, a stark contrast to the memories they held dear.

"You know," said Percy, breaking the silence, "this area has seen its share of history. The old desert trade routes, the ancient tribes... it's hard to imagine we're part of that story now".

"Hard to think about though when you're thirsty and exhausted," Boggy grumbled, "but I know what you mean. There's a strange kind of beauty to it all, even if it is trying to kill us!"

On the 1st of June the sky over the congested Brigade camp echoed to the rumbling sound of a lone German aircraft, which managed to drop six bombs, resulting in the loss of many men and horses, of the 3rd Light Horse, in the explosions, as well as a large proportion of the Brigade horses stampeding, many being lost forever in the desolate desert landscape. Following this raid, Brigades began dispersing their units while encamped in the desert.

Each regiment of the Light Horse began to take turns on rostered long range patrols, but Turkish patrols were rarely seen, as the Turks knew full well that the allied armies were out for revenge following the Easter raid.

Water was still scarce, and that, combined with moving supplies across the desert, limited the radius of patrols to twenty five miles from Romani.

Between the 10th and 12th of June, the 2nd Light Horse encountered a Turkish patrol whilst on a reconnaissance of Bir-Bay'Ud. Shots rang out as the two forces exchanged fire.

"Rip in to the bastards!" shouted Percy, as bullets whizzed past like blow flies.

The men all perched in their saddles and returned fire, their explosion of rounds enough to make the Turks flee.

"They're buggering off!" yelled Boggy, sweat dripping from his brow, but the horses were in no condition for a long pursuit, so the decision was made to hold their position and eventually withdraw, knowing the return journey to Romani would be arduous for their weary mounts.

The remainder of June saw the regiment patrolling Oghratina, Hod-El-Ge 'Elia, Mushalfat, and Bir-El-Mageibra, always vigilant and ready for the next skirmish.

"Let's hope the horses hold up," muttered Chugger, patting his exhausted steed as they moved out on yet another patrol.

Air raids too became a daily occurrence, and, each time, the horses were led away from the lines and scattered; a tactic that was working well.

5

Fight like Trojans and die like Spartans

Archie and Roo were constantly in Percy's thoughts, and he was disappointed that they had not had the chance to re-unite before the infantry was shipped out to France. But for Archie and Roo, their battles on the Western Front were about to begin in earnest when, on the 30th of May, the war in France had arrived without warning, commencing with an intense and sudden artillery bombardment, the brigade's first heavy shelling of the war; a hundred times worse than anything experienced on the peninsula.

As the shells began to rain down, the troops could hear the whistling of shells overhead, each man scrambling to find shelter in the trenches as the incoming artillery rounds created an ear-splitting row, causing the ground to shake violently with each explosion and sending showers of dirt and debris cascading down. The air too was thick with the acrid smell of gunpowder and the choking dust that settled in the aftermath of each shell, and during the lulls between bombardments, the men would quickly check on each other, ensuring no one was missing or injured, sharing whispered reassurances and gallows humour, which bolstered their spirits.

The battalion's first heavy shelling of the war was a baptism of fire; a brutal introduction to the horrors of the Western Front. But this was only the beginning, for as the guns fell silent, a sizeable force of German infantry appeared out of the dust and smoke, pushing aside the shattered barbed wire entanglements and leaping into the 11th Battalion positions on the left flank of the 9th.

Gunfire broke out all along the Australian front line as more enemy infantry poured across no man's land, shattering the stillness of the day, and echoing across the desolate expanse of land. Along the line, soldiers scrambled to respond to the unexpected onslaught, their hearts pounding with adrenaline-fuelled urgency. In an instant the Lewis Gun team were outed by the blast from an exploding mortar shell, their gun falling silent, but undamaged. Clancy and Roo were quick to notice the vital weapon being out of action, their mates lying unconscious in the trench, and rushed to the Lewis Gun position, dragging young Private Kropp with them.

The once boisterous and cocky Private Kropp was now shaking in his boots as rounds cracked and thumped overhead. The fear that he so confidently had dismissed, was upon him as he kept his head down and tried to aid the downed machine crew in an effort to avoid the battle. The crew was unconscious but otherwise unscathed.

"LEAVE THEM! THE BLOODY GERMANS ARE COMING...STRETCHER BEARER!" shouted Clancy.

"Righto boys let's refresh our memories a bit eh, but bloody quickly," said Clancy as he righted the gun and placed the butt in his shoulder, "Roo, you feed me the magazines, Kroppy, you load them...oh, and feel free to take a few pot shots too boys whilst I sort this gun out".

The Lewis Gun was a light machine gun which could be carried and operated by one man, unlike the much heavier Vickers. It was fitted with a pan magazine, basically a circular shape, which held forty seven rounds that were loaded with their noses pointing inwards facing the centre, in a radial fan. It was supported by a bipod at the front and by the firer's shoulder at the rear, and could fire five to six hundred rounds per minute.

As Clancy flicked up and adjusted the rear sight, Roo attached a full magazine.

"Don't forget Clance, bursts only, don't just let rip," Roo advised.

Clancy thought for a brief moment.

"Didn't Mac have a rhyme or something for that," he asked.

"Wasn't it bursts of three, two and two, I'll stuff you...before you...stuff me?" replied Roo.

"I don't think the word was 'stuff', but that'll do mate," laughed Clancy.

And so began the work of the machine gun; short bursts from left to right, then right to left, spraying death towards their enemy, as they fell like tin ducks at the fair.

"Look at the bastards drop!" shouted an excited Clancy.

Meanwhile Kropp was quivering at the bottom of the trench, and was soon noticed by an angry Sergeant Taylor.

"WHAT THE BLAZES?!" shouted Roo, "get up, load these mags and then start shooting. These buggers won't give a stuff if you're scared or not, so get at them!"

But Kropp did not move, frozen like a statue, secretly hoping that all of this was just a dream that he would soon wake up from.

"GET UP!" shouted Roo, as he grabbed Kropp and did his best to man handle him to his feet, "now get loading, or it won't be just the Germans you have to deal with".

Kropp scrambled to stand up, whilst Roo clipped a full magazine on to the machine gun.

As Clancy continued to fire, he detected a bit of an odour in the air and, between bursts, held out his hand to Roo.

"Ten bob I think mate...come on...hand it over," said Clancy.

"What? Right now?" replied Roo.

"No time like the present. Besides I could be dead in a mo, so want to savour being rich while I can," laughed the CSM.

Roo shook his head, then reached in to his breast pocket and produced a ten shilling note, which he promptly handed over to Clancy.

"Cheers Roo," said Clancy, smiling and sniffing the crisp bank note.

By this time, Kropp had come to his senses and had seen the exchange of money.

"What's the ten shillings for?" he enquired.

Clancy fired another burst at the now depleted enemy.

"We had a bet that you would either shit or piss yourself in your first fight," replied the CSM, "and, by the smell of you, *I* won".

Kropp felt embarrassed, but now saw both the humour and the irony of the situation.

"Well, you both won then," replied the rather sheepish soldier.

"Really? You beauty!" said Roo, hand outstretched to Clancy, "give!"

"You bastard," Clancy mumbled to himself, as he begrudgingly handed Roo back his money.

Private Kropp was now working fast reloading the machine gun magazines, but still felt ashamed. Roo was quick to notice.

"Hey, Kroppy. Chin up," said Roo, "I pissed *myself* on the first day at Gallipoli. In fact, so did the sergeant major here as I recall".

"Fair dinkum?" replied a surprised and slightly relieved Private Kropp.

"That's right Roo, tell him all my secrets," said Clancy with a cheeky wink and grin, "so remember Kroppy, you're not a true soldier until you fill your undies in battle".

"Shame about the ten bob though mate," added Roo.

As Clancy glanced at Kropp he said "not really. I think Ten Bob is a good name for our new mate here. What do you reckon?"

The large numbers of German soldiers now in the 11th Battalion trench were inflicting heavy losses on the occupants, who eventually were forced to withdraw to the flanks and rear, allowing the enemy to briefly occupy their abandoned positions. However, once the bombardment had slackened off, the 11th, assisted by the 9th, re-occupied the very badly battered and empty front line.

As the smoke and dust began to clear, Freddy and Tomo dropped into the trench.

"Good day chaps, how are you all?" asked Freddy.

"Good day? That's not very Astrayan is it?" said a disgruntled Clancy, "if you want to be a dinky di Aussie then it's g'day, how's it going?"

"Yeah, you did say you'd be talking like an Aussie by the end of all this," added Roo.

"Yes, well, it isn't over by a long shot just yet. In fact the big wigs think that it will be 1922 before we go home".

"1922? Bugger me!" exclaimed Clancy, "you'd better keep that one to yourself or the boys *will* be spewing".

"God help the Germans then, what?" replied Freddy.

From the machine gun position the five men looked on in astonishment as the German soldiers withdrew back through no man's land.

As the Germans fled towards their trenches, the Australians continued to fire at the retreating men. Scores of stammering machine guns and rifles erupted violently, their noise drowning out the distant artillery cannonade, the air thickened with bullets. Gaps appeared in the lines of fleeing men, some wide, some narrow, the survivors spreading out, trying to avoid the wall of lead coming at them from their rear. Bullets skimmed low, from knee to groin, cutting down men before they hit the ground, scores of men being felled in the blink of an eye, like rows of teeth knocked from a comb. Some of the wounded wriggled into shell holes or were struck again, many sliced in two by streams of bullets. Then all was still and quiet, apart from the sounds of rifle bolts pushing a fresh round forward into the chamber.

"What was the bloody point of that? Shell us, run in, then bugger off?!" exclaimed Clancy.

"Testing us out most likely," replied Captain Ponsonby, "but it rather reminds me of old Johnny Turk throwing thousands of men at us just to be shot down".

As the two men shook their heads Roo, trying to lighten the mood, pointed to a rather sheepish looking Private Kropp.

"Hey skip, have you met our new mate Ten Bob here?" he blurted out.

Clancy laughed out loud.

"Ten bob?" replied Ponsonby.

Roo shrugged his shoulders.

"Never mind, I'll tell you later…but he's a good bloke".

Summer time in France officially began on the 14th of June with all watches being advanced by one hour, and with the summer, came a new vigour for raids by the 1st ANZAC Corps on the German line. The main reason for the raids was intelligence gathering through the taking of prisoners, but also as a distraction to the preparations for a full scale allied assault to be launched in the area of the River Somme.

The 11th and 9th Battalions were designated to carry out two of these raids. Captain Wilder-Neligan was selected to command the 9th's raid, along with one hundred and sixty volunteers from the battalion. The raiding party was to be billeted in farmhouses between Sailly and Steenwerck, and, on arrival on the 11th of June, began practising in earnest for the stunt. The one hundred and sixty men were selected from the entire battalion, who had all put their hands up, hoping to get stuck in to the Hun. Freddy, Clancy, Archie, Roo, Stowie, Taff, Jacko, Tomo and Ten Bob Kropp were part of "the lucky few", as Shakespeare had written, and soon commenced detailed rehearsals for the raid.

Technology and aerial reconnaissance were beginning to play an important role in this new type of war, with mock up trenches being dug, based on aerial photographs of the target area. The attack was methodically contrived and practised to the letter, with each man knowing *his* part, and that of each attack party, in detail. The final numbers were fixed at four officers and one hundred and fifty one other ranks, plus three sappers from the Engineers. The attackers were divided in to three parties, with Ponsonby tagging along with Captain Benson, who was leading one of those parties, and Lieutenant Sargent in tow for a little bit of battle experience. The raid's objectives were the destruction of enemy material and equipment, intelligence gathering, and the encouragement of espirit de corps in the battalion; not that any more was required.

The raid was to be a complete surprise, consisting of a series of feints, and above all, no preparatory artillery barrage. The attack point was determined as being near Ru Du Bois, north east of the Sugar Loaf Salient, which was a pivotal point within the enemy territory, that posed a grave threat to the British and ANZAC forces. It was situated deep within enemy lines, and was a fortified stronghold bristling with numerous machine gun emplacements. It was perched on the high ground like a menacing spearhead protruding towards the allied lines, its strategic position bestowing upon the enemy an unparalleled advantage, dominating the surrounding terrain and casting a shadow of peril over any attempts to breach the ridge, and allowing it to unleash a devastating enfilading fire upon any advancing troops. The area of no man's land at this point was three hundred yards wide, but was specifically chosen in order to eliminate a troublesome enemy machine gun.

In order to distract the enemy from the battalion's true intentions, a feint bombardment would be launched on a section of the enemy line a quarter of a mile to the right. Also, in the days leading up to the attack, the trench mortars of the battalion expertly and methodically cut the enemy concertina wire to the front and at other points around the objectives.

Patrols were also sent out into no man's land, not only to convince the Germans that it was business as usual, but also for each attack leader to get to know the lay of the land, and thus avoid any surprises.

A battalion of the 5th Division temporarily occupied the line which had been the 9th's.

Although the men had rehearsed and rehearsed the raid, the troops were kept in complete ignorance of the target…until the early morning of the 2nd of July when the raiders were transported in motor lorries from their reserve positions to a ruined farmhouse just behind the front line. They had been briefed the night before, but today would carry out a final rehearsal.

Rehearsal successfully completed, there was much personal admin to carry out.

Captain Ponsonby and CSM McBride gathered their platoon together.

"Here you go boys, pass these around," said the CSM, as he tossed the men several tins of black boot polish.

Stowie looked at the polish in disgust.

"Another parade is it?" he asked.

"You silly bugger," said Clancy, "it's to black out your faces and bayonets so there is no shine in the dark mate".

"Oh...right...good idea," replied Stowie, feeling a bit foolish.

"Also," said Captain Ponsonby, "there are to be no personal or identifying articles taken on the raid, so remove all unit insignias, identity discs; and no pay books. We don't want old Fritz knowing who he has to his front".

Next Clancy passed around packs of chewing gum, which confused the troops even more.

"If you chew this when on the move, it will stop you from coughing, and giving us away," the CSM explained, "or so the MO says".

Much nodding of heads signalled that the men understood.

"They've thought of everything," Taff whispered to Roo.

The time of the attack was set for 2350 hours. All parties moved to the forming up point on the parapet and began their departure through the sally port, which was essentially a closely guarded opening in the trench wall, designed for the quick passage of troops.

The night was dark and moonless as the three groups moved stealthily towards no man's land, nervously ruminating on their issued chewing gum. Benson and Ponsonby's party began to fan out on the right flank when, without warning, a soldier in the centre began to cough uncontrollably. The entire party froze in their tracks, many dropping down on one knee, others lying prostrate.

"So much for the chewing gum," said Kropp in a low voice, but he was cut short by an annoyed whisper from the CSM.

"BLOODY SHUT UP!"

He did.

The coughing man was sent packing the fifty yards back to the start point, much to the relief of all, in disbelief that there had been no reaction from the enemy.

By forty minutes after midnight all three groups were in no man's land, separated by a distance of two hundred yards from one another, and approximately two hundred yards from the enemy front line.

The next part of the plan was set in motion. The raiders now needed to make a mad dash to within fifty yards of the German trenches, but the sound of a hundred and sixty pairs of hobnail boots simultaneously striding across the uneven terrain is something even Clancy's deaf old granny, as he had put it, would be able to hear. The answer, two machine guns in the ANZAC trenches were now firing bursts beyond the flanks of the raiders in order to drown out the noise.

The three party commanders, almost at the same time, raised

and lowered their hands. This was the signal to sprint forward, and, as it rippled down the line, each man began their rapid advance into the darkness, as the machine guns did their work.

Although it was pitch black the three groups managed to keep their bearings towards the enemy...to a fashion.

Lieutenant Young kept the left hand party true by watching a tower which stood to the rear of the enemy positions. Although it was dark, the tower's silhouette stood out like a beacon in the night.

Despite the mortars managing to cut the barbed wire, both the left and centre parties were met by newly placed entanglements. The troops, quietly and methodically, beat down the wire as best as they could, and then handed over to the Mat Men, who carried twelve foot long canvass mats which were mounted on a base of wire netting. No sooner was the wire discovered, as per their many rehearsals, the Mat Men ran forward and expertly placed the mats on it; then over went the raiders.

Benson and Ponsonby's right hand party had a better time of it, reaching the fifty yard line without incident.

With all raiding parties in position, the hard work of the battalion signallers came into their own. During the advance, the signallers had been laying a communication line for the field telephone, and now it was time for the telephone call to the artillery and machine guns. At approximately 0230 hours Captain Wilder-Neligan telephoned the Fire Control Centre and uttered the codeword 'Gallop', confirming that all parties were safe on their final positions. Within thirty seconds the machine guns on both flanks opened fire and began to spit lead in to the darkness, whilst twenty minutes later the artillery laid down a terrifying barrage beyond the German positions. As the shells whined overhead and exploded in the near distance, the old sweats from the original battalion became suddenly aware that this theatre of war was a lot different to what they had experienced at Gallipoli, marvelling at the destructive light show to their front.

Each man was wearing a white calico armband with a stripe of luminous paint around the centre. These were for identification purposes once the physical attack was underway, but had been covered with a piece of hessian until the time came.

There was no need to whisper any more, as the machine guns rattled and the artillery shells screamed overhead, bursting in a wall of fire just behind the German trenches. The breastwork of the enemy line was eight feet deep. Before the artillery bombardment the forward line was sparsely manned for the night, but it was now full to the brim with soldiers who had moved from the rear and flanks to escape the deadly barrage. The enemy were now awake and firing into the darkness, expecting the inevitable rush of British infantrymen.

As the order came for the raiders to remove the hessian from their armbands, the German's new adversary in the form of strapping battle hardened Aussies was on its way to say "g'day".

The element of surprise had gone, for the stage had been set by the big guns. Each party surged across no man's land, a desperate sprint towards the enemy, with the lingering hope that the enemy were still reeling from the relentless barrage of artillery shells that had pounded their positions, in preparation for the grim dance on the battlefield.

But today was about reputation, about instilling fear of the

ANZACs in to the German soldiers. Soldiers die. Everyone dies. But reputation lives forever and that was why, as they ran, many of the men screamed "AUSTRALIA!" in the hope of etching the word in to the minds of those who stood against them. As the Aussies dropped in to the enemy trenches some even inexplicably screamed their own names and those of loved ones and fallen mates, not knowing why; perhaps out of comfort or revenge.

Sergeant Major McBride landed with a thud in the slippery trench, shouting out "I'M CLANCY OF THE OVERFLOW YOU BASTARDS!!!" as his bayonet took its first soul. His victim was a medium built fellow, wearing a battered helmet, and clutching a Gewehr 98 rifle fitted with a fourteen and a half inch long saw back, or butchers blade, bayonet, a blade with a ghastly reputation of disembowelling a victim when removed. The German instinctively thrust his bayonet towards Clancy who, just as instinctively, parried his lunge with the stock of his rifle, before inserting his own blade in to the German soldier's throat. Next Clancy shoulder charged a man to his left, knocking him to the ground then stamping on his groin, whilst his rifle fended off a bayonet swing from his right side. He then calmly stepped over the man whose groin was now a bloodied mangle of flesh, making his way along the trench seeking out more enemies to kill. "BASTARDS!!" he shouted, with blood curdling vigour, as he drove in to the enemy. He seemed to be inviting death, for at that moment he was immortal, as were all of the raiders as they unleashed death. Time appeared to have slowed and the Germans were snail like in their speed, but the Aussies were faster, stabbing, thrusting, slashing, until the trench floor ran with a river of blood.

Clancy was still shouting as his bayonet lunged in to a man's eye, driving hard until the tip of the blade burst through the back of the soldier's skull. He stepped right as he tried to shake the bayonet loose from his victim's head, only just avoiding a bayonet coming straight for *his* face, then watching as the point of an Aussie blade suddenly broke through his would be killer's chest.

As Roo kicked the dead German loose from his bayonet he shouted to Clancy.

"FIRE A ROUND OFF!"

"WHAT?" replied Clancy, struggling to hear his mate through the chaos and mayhem that engulfed them.

"FIRE A BLOODY ROUND OFF TO FREE YOUR BAYONET," shouted Roo.

Clancy suddenly came to his senses. He was the Company Sergeant Major, but in the heat of the moment his mind was a blank and his training had left him. "If your bayonet gets stuck just fire a round off and that will do the trick" he had drilled in to the men during their many training sessions.

"Bloody hell! Thanks Roo," said Clancy, looking a little sheepish. Then the fire was back in his eyes.

BANG! The deafening shot echoed through the chaos, the dead German's head disintegrating, fragments scattering in all directions. Clancy stumbled backwards as his bayonet was released with a sudden jolt. The battlefield seethed with the intensity of the deadly struggle as Roo reached out, seizing Clancy's hand and hoisting him to his feet. Though the urgency to rejoin the fight pressed upon them, they found themselves momentarily fixated on the headless German, a macabre sight that held them in a stunned pause, a pause cut short by a familiar voice.

"Come on you fellows, you can admire your work later...oh dear..." said Captain Ponsonby, as his eyes beguiled the gruesome sight that lay before them.

Clancy, although still stunned, acknowledged his mate.

"G'day Freddie. Bit of a mess eh?" he said.

"The whole place is a mess, but there is more to clean up, so to speak," replied Freddie, "have you seen Archie and the others?"

"They were a few yards to my right as we ran in so must be up there somewhere," replied Roo, pointing along the trench.

Freddie waved his pistol in the air.

"Well there is no time like the present eh? Once more in to the breach and all that," said the Captain enthusiastically, as he, Clancy and Roo rejoined the fray.

About thirty yards to their right, Archie was swinging his rifle round like a mad man, stabbing with his bayonet, and clubbing with his rifle butt. Stowie meanwhile was tossing mills bombs in to dugouts, then taking careful aim as enemy soldiers rushed out in to the trench, downing each one in fast succession. Dugout clear, Stowie turned his rifle's attention to any unobstructed shots he had of the enemy fighting in the trench. But danger lurked everywhere, a dazed German soldier, armed with a wooden plank, appearing from the dugout to Stowie's rear, slicing the air with the piece of wood. A sudden wind swished above Stowie's head as the German swung the plank at him, missing. As quick as a flash, the Texan spun round, dropped to his knees and pushed his bayonet hard forward to pierce the woollen tunic of the plank wielding soldier. Stowie twisted his rifle so that the bayonet would not be seized by the man's belly while it gouged his blood and guts. The soldier staggered back as Stowie's bayonet was pulled free from his belly and flew wide to crash firmly against another bayonet, which Stowie followed whilst calling out "REMEMBER THE ALAMO".

As he screamed, he saw the terror on his new enemy's face, and terror on an enemy breeds savagery and death.

"TEXAS!!" shouted Stowie, as he stared at him.

The man saw death coming and he tried to back away, but Archie was there and blocked his retreat, whilst Stowie smiled as he slashed his bayonet across the German's face. Blood sprayed bright red in the darkness, as the blade's backswing sliced the soldier's throat. Blood gurgled and the man's eyes almost popped from his head, as he grasped his throat, then fell to the ground, dead.

During the advance through the smoke and haze, Captain Wilder-Neligan had encountered an enemy OP to the front of the parapet. He immediately spied three enemy soldiers and dispatched two with his revolver, but the third managed to toss a bomb in his direction, the shrapnel wounding him in the head and shoulder. Despite his injuries he carried on in to the enemy trench.

The fighting may have been intense, but the Aussies had their own enterprising ways in dealing with Fritz. Some, like Private Cunningham, tossed aside their weapons temporarily and used their fists to knock down their opponents. Even Captain

Ponsonby had a go at boxing the enemy's ears, much to the delight of his mates.

"That's it Freddy, give 'em what for," shouted a smiling Clancy as he kicked a German soldier between the legs, "it's just like the boozer on a Friday night".

In the mean time Lieutenant Sargent had located a large dugout which he suspected contained enemy soldiers. Poking his pistol through the hessian curtain, he fired several rounds in to the shelter then tossed in a mills bomb for good measure.

Archie was soon by his side.

"Here Tomo, let's try this," he uttered to his officer.

Archie had fitted an electric torch to the stock of his rifle and now shone the bright white beam down into the dugout, revealing a crowd of Germans huddled together in a corner. Both sides paused momentarily as they decided what to do, but in a split second a German officer had raised his pistol and fired a round in Archie's direction. The round missed and both Archie and Tomo returned fire, with several shots, using the torch beam as a guide. It was so easy that Archie just fired from the hip, for wherever the light went, the bullets were sure to follow.

Roo and Clancy soon appeared and gazed down into the dugout which was now strewn with fifteen bodies.

"Like shooting fish in a barrel eh boys?" shouted the CSM as he patted both men on the shoulder, "now come on there's more work to be done".

Captain Young's party on the left had encountered light resistance, quickly dealing with them, including a signaller who had been speaking on the field telephone before his conversation was violently cut short. They did, however, locate the machine gun that they were seeking. It was a "big bastard", heavy and mounted on a tripod, but the men managed to lift and carry it back to the Aussie lines.

Over on the right flank the red mist of battle had led to almost all those who resisted being killed, with only four prisoners being taken.

Each party had two Tape Men whose job it was to mark a withdrawal route with white mine tape. The tape had been laid from the enemy breastwork, the Tape Men then retiring to the enemy parapet to await the signal for all to return.

When the time to withdraw was finally announced by the firing of a single rocket by the CO, the Tape Men came into their own, guiding the attackers to the taped lane whilst madness and confusion reigned around them, shouting out "Imshee! This way! This way!"

Other soldiers too called out "Imshee!" along the German line to ensure all knew that it was time to withdraw.

Amidst the chaos, the raiding parties executed a meticulously planned and ordered withdrawal, their movements synchronised amidst the thunder of gunfire and explosions. Each soldier knew their role, their rehearsals over the past few days guiding their actions as they navigated the treacherous terrain, maintaining their discipline and providing covering fire for one another as they made their way back towards their own lines, whilst bullets whizzed past them, kicking up dirt at their feet.

Freddy, Clancy and Captain Benson waited until last to ensure that everyone made it back. The last man finally through, the three men joined the withdrawing troops down the taped laneway, but as they approached the barbed wire entanglements they encountered two wounded ANZACs leaning against a wooden post.

"Can you walk?" asked Benson.

"No sir," replied one man, as his mate lay moaning in the dirt.

Clancy and Freddy instinctively grabbed both men and flung them across their shoulders. As they did so a burst of machine gun fire rang out from the German lines, and Captain Benson fell to the ground...dead. The two men stared momentarily at the lifeless officer, until there was a sudden rat tat tat from behind, followed by the stirring and flinging about of dirt and dust, as the enemy machine gunner searched blindly in the darkness for his next mark.

"RUN YER BUGGER, RUN!" shouted Clancy, as the two men, carrying their human cargo, ran like a spooked stallion towards the retiring attack parties.

The dead German signaller, it transpired, had left the Aussies a parting gift before meeting his own demise, for, as the three groups were two thirds of the way across no man's land, a German artillery barrage fell on *them* and also in the gap *between* them and the ANZAC front line. Order turned to chaos as the men scattered to avoid the incoming shells. Some, including a party of another fifteen prisoners who had been rounded up in no man's land, and their escort, noticed what appeared to be a large drainage ditch, which turned out to be the River Laies, running parallel with the ANZAC line, and all took shelter in it, whilst waiting for their moment to dash the final few yards to safety.

As Clancy and Freddy emerged from the darkness, they lowered the wounded soldiers in to the trench then paused at the parapet, exchanging a wordless glance, their figures silhouetted against the glow of explosions in no man's land. They stood side by side, shoulders squared and gazes fixed ahead, waiting patiently for their men to return.

As the last of the soldiers finally made their way back, the two men nodded in silent satisfaction; their men were accounted for, their mission accomplished. But even as they turned to drop in to their trench, the two men remained ever vigilant, their senses attuned to the dangers that lurked in the darkness. For in war, the safety of one's men always came first, even if it meant facing personal peril in the process.

By 0330 hours everyone was safely back in friendly lines. Ten men had been killed in the raid and another two died later from their wounds. Another twenty eight had been wounded; this number included Captain Wilder-Neligan the OC of the raid who, despite his wounds, had remained at his post. Most of the casualties had been sustained during the enemy artillery bombardment in no man's land.

The returning troops sat for a moment on the floor of the forward trench, getting their breath back, and coming back to reality after a bloodthirsty night. As they rested, a group of German prisoners began to file past them. Amongst them was a soldier wearing a Pickelhaube, an old-style helmet with a spike on top. The Pickelhaube had been replaced with their now familiar steel helmet earlier that year, the new helmet earning the Germans the nickname "Square Heads" from their Aussie counterparts; so this old helmet was a rare sight and piqued the Australians' interest.

"What the hell have you got on your head? Mind if I relieve you of it, mate?" Archie quipped.

The German soldier looked up, weariness in his eyes, replying in English.

"It is an old helmet, not used anymore. You like it?" asked the soldier as he passed the helmet to Archie for a closer inspection.

"Bloody hell, this is as good as a bayonet in a trench fight," Roo commented, examining the helmet.

"Yeah, that spike is a weapon in itself," noted Clancy.

As he admired the helmet, Archie reached into his tunic pocket and pulled out three packets of cigarettes.

"I don't smoke mate so these are no good to me. Would you accept them in trade for the helmet?" he asked.

The German soldier hesitated for a moment before nodding and handing it over, gladly accepting the cigarettes.

"It is not good anyway," he said, "it is made of...er...kuh...er...leder".

"Leder? Oh...leather?" replied Archie as he tried to translate the German's words.

"Ja...leather," replied the German, nodding, "it does not protect well against shrapnel, but the spike, many years ago, was to stop a sword strike to the head. Danke, Australia".

"I'm Archie. Your English is very good," said Archie.

"I am Martin, Martin Titzica," replied the soldier, reaching out to shake Archie's hand.

"Thanks Martin...and good luck to you," replied Archie gladly grasping Martin's hand just as the prisoners were ushered away.

"Titzica...that's not a very German sounding name," said Clancy.

"Yeah, well, McBride is a Scottish name and you don't sound much like a jock do you? Besides, how many Germans do *you* know?" replied Archie.

Clancy scratched his head for a moment.

"Good point mate".

"What are you going to do with that mate?" asked Roo as he gazed at the German helmet.

"I'm going to send it home to Mum and Dad as soon as we are back in the rear," Archie replied.

Raid complete, it was back on the trucks to the Division baths at Bac St Maur, followed by a coffee and rum issue. The veterans were very grateful for the luxuries which were being lavished upon them, but most revelled in silence, pondering over their night's work.

"Well, that was new," said Archie.

"What the attack?" asked Tomo, "yes it was. I have never killed anyone before".

Archie and Clancy ignored Tomo's comment, trying to put the raid and those that they had killed out of their thoughts.

"Next we'll be having tea and scones," joked Clancy.

"Ooh, aunty Doris makes beautiful scones," replied Roo, licking his lips with thoughts of home.

"I've been informed that we can all sleep for the rest of the day," announced Freddy.

"Really?" asked a surprised Roo, "what's this war coming to?"

Lieutenant Sargent looked around at his friends and smiled and laughed awkwardly at the conversations which surrounded him. It appeared to be a normal day to them, and the horror and violence which they had all seen and committed did not seem to have even happened. Freddy, noticing that the young lieutenant seemed lost and confused, placed his hand on his shoulder.

"Cheer up Tommy, we survived, that's what matters," said Freddy.

Tomo quickly glanced around at his comrades.

"Look at them. Not a care in the world. We might as well have just been for a stroll in the park or something," he replied.

"It's just their...no...it's *our* way of dealing with it. You. Me. Everyone here. Of course it plays on our minds, but you just have to put it aside or you'll go mad," said Freddy, "but I have no doubt that one day it will all come back to haunt us".

The next day the 9th Battalion marched out to Oultersteeve for a week of training and rest, then it was on to Berthen and Godewaersvelde, from where they entrained to a destination unknown, on the 10th of July, passing through Hazebrouck and St Pol, arriving at Doullens at 0300 hours.

Their well deserved sleep in their horse carriages, as it turned out, had been a godsend, for, on disembarking the train, there followed a nine hour march to Halloy-Les-Pernois, and after a nights rest in billets in the village of Canaples, the battalion moved to Naours, situated nine miles north of Amiens, and nineteen miles behind the front lines. The battalion was now within a cooee distance from the Somme.

"Blimey, I think I've seen more of France and Belgium than I have the whole of Queensland!" remarked Clancy.

The 1st, 2nd and 4th Australian Divisions now formed the 1st ANZAC Corps under the command of General Gough.

Between marches and rest stops, on the 13th of July, the battalion was issued with the new box respirators which replaced the old and uncomfortable PH Gas Helmet. The new respirator fitted on the wearers head and had a canvas bag suspended from it, which contained a filter and a substance to eliminate the gas.

"Finally; this is much better," said Stowie, as he tried on his new respirator, "I was getting tired of that old one squeezing my head...how do I look?"

Clancy said nothing, managing a chuckle to himself.

"Yeah, this one actually feels like it was made with us in mind," Roo agreed, as he admired the canvas bag, "and it's much more comfortable".

"It's a strange looking thing but it makes me feel a bit safer," added Archie.

Someone must have had a premonition about the new respirators for, at the town of Contalmaison eight days later, the battalion was greeted with a gas attack, their first initiation in to this type of warfare. Their training had served them well, with each man masking in good time, and no casualties.

Having arrived at 0200 hours, minus blankets and packs, a sure sign of an impending battle, the battalion was billeted in old German trenches in what was known as Sausage Valley.

When the sun rose, the daylight revealed a pock marked landscape of craters of all sizes. Unexploded ordnance and enemy equipment was strewn everywhere, and the unmistakable odour of rotting, unburied bodies hovered in the air.

"I remember that smell very well," said Roo as he thought about the bodies strewn across their front for weeks at Gallipoli.

Clancy looked around and saw that the town of Contalmaison

was a pile of rubble, except for part of a house which stood alone as a reminder that people had once lived here.

"This is how I always imagined Hell to look like," he uttered.

"Well, it may not *be* Hell, but it has certainly been through it a few times," Roo added.

"Ey up...here comes trouble," said Taff as he saw Captain Ponsonby making his way along the trench towards them.

"Morning skipper," said Clancy, noticing a serious and determined expression on the Captain's face.

"CSM, please tell the chaps to dump all unnecessary kit over there," announced the officer, "the CQMS will collect it and store it somewhere safe".

Suddenly the ears of all veterans in earshot pricked up, for "dump your kit" only meant one thing to them...there's a battle coming.

Clancy noticed many smiles turn to worry.

"Come on fellas. Are we downhearted?" he asked.

The atmosphere perked up as the CSM received the group reply of "NO!" as the men began stacking their packs in a neat pile, and singing the song that the CSM had just quoted.

"Not while Britannia rules the waves..."

As the troops beavered away they encouraged the new lads to join in.

"That worked a treat Sergeant Major," said Ponsonby, as he placed his hand on Clancy's shoulder.

"Always happy to do my bit for morale mate," replied the CSM.

Whilst the 9th Battalion had been rehearsing for their earlier trench raid, a huge British and French offensive had begun on the 1st of July along a front line of twenty three miles. The attackers were thirteen British and five French divisions, operating to the north and south of the River Somme. Heavy losses by the French around Verdun had resulted in the original plan of sixty four divisions attacking on a forty five mile front to be drastically altered. The first day of the battle was the bloodiest day in the history of the British Army, with the British suffering fifty seven thousand four hundred and twenty casualties; nineteen thousand two hundred and forty of whom were killed.

Bapaume, an agricultural town, was one of the final objectives due to its strategic position as a crossing point between Artois and the Flanders plain on one side, and the Somme valley and the Paris Basin on the other. But, despite success in the southern section, the offensive was more or less a failure, with the British advance stalling at a position in front of the town of Pozieres.

Pozieres, a small town of less than two hundred inhabitants, itself was a significant part of the main plan, for it sat on high ground, amidst rolling hills and agricultural fields, with an all round view of the surrounding countryside; excellent for observation posts and artillery spotters. The area of the Somme was no stranger to war, for in 1346 during the Hundred Years War, The Battle of Crécy took place here, between a French and an English army, resulting in a French defeat, when they attacked the English whilst they were traversing northern France. What was now occurring would make the medieval battle appear like a small skirmish.

The direction of the allied advance was towards Bapaume, but in order to get there the towns of Pozieres, and Thiepval, to the north west had to be taken. The British army had made three failed attempts, with severe losses, to capture Pozieres, so now it was up to the 1st Australian Division to have a go; the ANZACs attacking the village in the centre, whilst imperial divisions advanced on the flanks.

An ancient Roman road ran south west to north west in a straight line from Albert, through Pozieres, to Bapaume. A ridge lay approximately a quarter of a mile beyond Pozieres, and on that ridge was a fortress like, and, seemingly impenetrable, double trench system known as the Old German lines, or OG1 and 2. The system stretched from the Somme to the River Ancre some nineteen miles distant. The remains of a windmill, which had stood proudly for three hundred years, was perched on the summit of the ridge, just behind OG2 on the northern side of the Roman road, towering menacingly, like a giant, over the countryside.

The British lines could be approached via Sausage Valley, from where two sunken roads led towards Pozieres. One of the roads began at the worryingly named Casualty Corner, whilst the other led from the village of Contalmaison. The Casualty Corner route led to 'K' Trench, beginning at the south west corner of the town and north past Pozieres cemetery on the right of the road from Albert.

The 9th were the lead battalion, taking the Australians into the area via Sausage Valley on the 20th of July. Each man had his soldier face on, a stern, resolute expression. There was no more singing, just a steady stride of determination as they moved forward down the valley, the only sound being the rhythmic squelch of boots in mud and the occasional rattle of their equipment.

The soldiers moved in unison, a disciplined and well trained battalion, their faces set with grim resolve, each step forward bringing them closer to the impending clash, the landscape around them a graphic reminder of the war's relentless march. As they progressed along the trench, the oppressive silence was broken only by the distant sounds of artillery and the occasional shouted order. The valley, once a serene stretch of land, now felt ominous under the weight of their collective thoughts and fears.

'A' and 'B' companies were to be the first in to the line, both companies being briefed by their respective OCs.

As the men huddled together in some dead ground between Brigade Headquarters at Contalmaison and the entrance to Black Watch Avenue, each man was given extra ammunition and a handful of Mills Bombs. Captain Ponsonby informed them of their intended route along Black Watch Avenue, where they were to relieve a company of the Staffordshire Regiment..

Both Roo and Archie's ears pricked up at the news.

"The Staffordshire Regiment? I wonder if Uncle Sam is with them?" said Archie.

Private Samuel Ford had been at Gallipoli, but Roo and Archie had not managed to cross paths with him there; Percy, however, had.

"How will we recognise him? We've never even met him," asked Roo.

Archie shrugged his shoulders.

"I don't know. Let's just hope he is still around to meet," he replied.

It was quite a hike to where the Staffords were located and, on arrival, the Englishmen whispered a cheer to the Aussies, which instilled a sense of gratitude, renewed vigour, and confidence in the 9th.

"G'day poms!" Clancy whispered, as he shook hands with anyone within reach.

"Ow do colonials, ow am yer?" came a reply, in the strange Black Country accent.

"Good thanks cobber," replied Roo, "hey, do any of you blokes know Samuel Ford?"

"Ar, I do," replied one of the soldiers, "ow do yow know Sam ar kid?"

Roo quickly deciphered the English soldier's words.

"Oh, he's mine and Archie here's uncle," Roo replied, pointing at his cousin.

The Englishman's eyes nearly popped out of his skull as he thrust his right hand forward, then grabbed both men in a bear hug.

"Well blow me darn. *I'm* Sam Ford, so yow must be Archie and Rueben. I met yower kid Percy at Suvla Bay yow know, and yow'm all sergeants too eh?" said a surprised and cheery Sam.

"Yeah, he told us in a letter," replied Archie, "I can't believe you are here. Mum *will* be pleased when I write and tell her".

The order came for the men from Staffordshire to move out of the line. The three men quickly scribbled down regimental numbers and units, and swapped pieces of paper.

"Send me a note when yow con lads. I ay gonna be far away, so it wo be the old snail mail," said Sam.

The three men shook hands and gave each other one last hug.

"Look after yourself uncle Sam, and we'll see you again; keep an eye out for the 9th Battalion AIF," said Archie.

"Yow too lads; yow too. Bless yer both," replied Sam as he joined his company and marched south west along Black Watch Avenue.

As the Staffords headed out, men in both units shook hands and wished each other well.

Once the officers and their counterparts had met and briefed one another, the two companies were left alone to man their position. As the artillery boomed almost constantly in the distance, each man was again left in their own thoughts, pondering their future.

Black Watch Avenue was connected to OG1 at a T junction. Parts of OG1 and 2 were in allied hands, with the enemy holding the remainder to the north. Pozieres trench, approximately seven hundred yards to the north of Black Watch Avenue and south of the village, was to be the first objective. It was indeed a perilous one, as it was bordered on its eastern end by the enemy held northern half of OG 1 and 2, as well as Munster Alley, another trench line on the right flank of OG2. This was the area that had been unsuccessfully attacked by the British at the beginning of July.

The Australian assault was set to kick off on the 23rd of July, and the 9th could see that they had much work and reconnaissance to do. The officers briefed their men on the task ahead.

As the men worked on getting comfortable, and improving

their trenches, there was much time for chatting and swapping of opinions.

"We are much better soldiers than these Tommies" announced Private Kropp.

The Gallipoli men paused at this sweeping statement by this new bloke.

"What?" exclaimed a surprised Roo.

"Well, I hear that the English regiments that went to Gallipoli weren't that good," replied Kropp.

"Really?" Clancy responded in disgust, "how would *you* know, you weren't *bloody* there!"

"Yes boyo, the British did their bit and lost loads of blokes. Some of their senior officers weren't much cop, but the men, well they were top blokes," added Taff.

"Take a look around you laddy. Can you not see what the British troops over here have done? What they have sacrificed. Are you blind?" said Clancy, "I cannot tell you how much I admire the English, Scotch, and Irish troops".

Archie coughed under his breath.

"It's Scottish not Scotch".

"Eh?" replied Clancy.

"Scotch is a drink…you know…whisky," Archie explained.

"And don't forget the Welsh," added Taff.

Clancy waived off the comments.

"Yeah, yeah…*you*, young Ten Bob, need to think before you start yabbering on. You are only as good as the man next to you".

Stowie could see that the conversation was getting heated.

"What about Gallipoli and France?" he interrupted.

"What do you mean?" asked Clancy.

"Well, some say that Gallipoli was a picnic compared to France, whilst others say that France is a picnic to Gallipoli," replied Stowie.

Apart from the distant artillery and small arms fire, all went quiet whilst the group pondered.

"It depends," Archie piped up.

"Depends? On what?" replied Stowie.

"Well at Gallipoli the hills made a position hard to take and easy to keep. But we were under fire for eight months, had no comforts, saw no civilisation, got little news, were couped up with very little freedom of movement, and the snipers and shells could get men just about anywhere," said Archie, "but here we are better fed, can buy what we like, read the latest in the English newspapers most days, see civilisation and move about with plenty of freedom".

Clancy shook his head and rolled his eyes.

"Yeah it sure is a picnic here…what's a bayonet in the guts between mates eh?"

"More like in the face as I recall," said Roo.

The men carried on digging.

As OG1 and 2 were running parallel to each other and formed part of both the German and Australian lines, preparations needed to be put in to action to be able to use this to the battalion's advantage. That said, on the evening of the 20th, Lieutenant Armstrong and his party excavated a trench which linked Black Watch Avenue, OG1 and OG2. Thus there was now a safe corridor to OG2.

That same evening Lieutenant Biggs, with Lieutenant Sargent in tow for the experience, gathered together twenty men, including Roo, Taff, Stowie and Jacko, to recce the area of the battalion front line situated one hundred and fifty yards ahead. As they moved through the darkness, checking to see if the enemy had erected any wire entanglements, Roo heard a shuffling noise, and soon noticed a German soldier hurriedly crawling back to his lines. Roo instinctively held up his hand to signal a halt, and dropped to his knees, followed by the rest of the group.

Lieutenant Biggs slowly worked his way towards Roo and whispered.

"What is it sergeant?"

"I just saw a German crawling back that way," he replied, pointing towards the town.

"Must have been an OP," replied the officer, as he surveyed the vast expanse of barbed wire entanglements to their front, "but we now know that there *is* wire out here, so I think we need to withdraw to from whence we came".

No sooner had Biggs spoken, enemy flares began bursting overhead, lighting up the darkness. Luckily the party had already squatted low and reduced their silhouette, so were difficult to spot in the flickering shadows created by the descending flares. Nonetheless the Germans, not shy to remove a few players from the field, began tossing bombs and firing machine guns in the area they thought the patrol was in. Lieutenant Biggs signalled to all to lie flat on their bellies, then, in pairs, the men crawled from shell hole to shell hole, making it safely back to Black Watch Avenue unscathed.

Lieutenant Biggs was grateful to Roo for his keen eyed observation.

"Good work Sergeant Taylor".

In the early hours of the 22nd, the probing attacks began, the idea being to keep the enemies' heads down by dropping a barrage of mortar bombs on their post, then to attack whilst an artillery barrage was directed just beyond the objective. Two parties of bombers were sent out from the OGs along with a few battalion Lewis Gun groups. The attack was supposed to commence at 0230 hours with the mortar barrage beginning at 0155 hours in order to disorientate the Germans and keep their heads down for thirty five minutes. Due to a supply error, however, the barrage was intermittent and ceased at 0210 hours, the reason, each mortar crew had only been issued with fourteen rounds of ammunition. Despite this mistake the two bombing parties led by Lieutenants Monteath and Biggs ventured out forty yards to await the artillery strike. Artillery had been landing off and on now all over the line, so it was hard to distinguish whether or not *their* barrage was occurring.

"Do you think that's our barrage?" Biggs whispered, peering into the darkness.

Monteath shook his head, frustration evident on his face.

"Hard to tell with all this noise, and the fact that shells are dropping all over the place".

Unsure, and growing impatient, Monteath jumped on the field telephone to Major Salisbury, the officer in charge of the attack.

"Major Salisbury, this is Monteath. I can see no distinguishable barrage."

There was a pause before Salisbury's voice crackled through. "Understood…both parties are to carry on in regardless".

Slightly relieved, Monteath relayed the orders to his men, a tenacious look crossing his face.

"Alright, lads, we're going in. Stay alert and stick to the plan."

Biggs nodded; a mix of resolve and apprehension in his eyes.

"Let's hope the rest of the operation goes smoother than this start."

Monteath's party advanced to discover that the enemy trench had been obliterated and was unrecognisable as a defensive position. The enemy, however, had not fallen back and began to bomb the Aussies, many becoming casualties. The Aussies returned the favour but were soon running low on Mills Bombs. Sergeant Browne, who was in support in Black Watch Avenue, saw their predicament and leapt out of the trench with a sack full of bombs, and began a deadly dash diagonally across the open ground. A burst of machine gun fire immediately cut him down.

Lieutenant Biggs's group came under a similar bombing barrage and withering fire from German machine guns. Eventually Sergeant Hodgson was the last man standing and quickly grabbed his wounded officer and ran through machine gun fire back to the safety of the Aussie lines.

Both attacks failed, with a loss of nine killed and twenty two wounded.

Despite these setbacks the battalion was feeling as mean as a blow fly in a brown paper bag. Payback was coming!

During the day much was going on in the Aussie trenches, resupply, ammo checks, eating and sleeping, and all whilst a continuous array of artillery shells screamed and whined overhead, slamming unceremoniously into the German positions.

"They reckon after all this we should be able to just walk over there," said an optimistic Jacko.

"Don't believe everything you hear mate. That's what the Tommies were told on the first day and look what happened to them," replied Corporal Stowe.

Clancy and Ponsonby were soon in the company lines, having worked their way, slipping and sliding, along Black Watch Avenue, from the Battalion Headquarters situated in OG1.

"Orders group. All NCOs on me and the captain," Clancy called down the line.

As the Platoon Sergeants and Section Commanders gathered around, each was impatient for the off. As Archie pulled his notebook and pencil from his breast pocket, he licked the sharpened end of his pencil.

"Well skip, what's the gossip?" he asked.

"The gossip, as Sergeant Taylor so aptly put it, my antipodean mates, is thus," said Captain Ponsonby, as he unfurled his map and gave it to Clancy to hold up, "tomorrow we attack Pozieres. There are three objectives. Pozieres trench here, the enemy second line in this orchard here, and the south east side of the old Roman road just here".

"Nothing much then sir," joked Stowie.

Ponsonby glanced at Corporal Stowe with a glint in his eye.

"No, just a walk on the beach eh boys," he replied.

The captain explained the details of how the attack would go in, with the 1st Brigade attacking on the left and the 3rd Brigade on the right.

"*Our* battalion's position is here on this four hundred and fifty yard stretch on the right. We will line up at the jumping off position here. The artillery will release the biggest barrage of the war so far, at 0030 hours, on objective number one, for two minutes; then they will redirect to objective two and so on. Then it's *our* turn," said the captain.

"The biggest barrage yet eh? Maybe Jacko here is right," said Stowie.

"Don't count your chickens mate," Clancy added.

"Any questions?" Ponsonby asked, as he glanced over to the CSM.

There was silence as all present began putting notebooks back in to pockets.

"Right lads; get your blokes back on sentry as per usual stags. Make sure everyone is fed, watered and gets some sleep…oh…and extra ammo and bombs will be issued shortly. Good luck eh boys. Be ready to go at 2330 hours," said Clancy as he checked his watch.

Like a well oiled machine the battalion formed up ready to go. Due to the shortage of armbands each man was told to roll their sleeves up to their elbows. Bayonets were quietly fixed to rifles, and each man was issued with a phosphorous grenade to be used for clearing out enemy dugouts.

"Be careful with these things fellas," said Roo, "it ignites when it comes in contact with the air and you can only stop it burning by submerging the affected part in water and picking it off".

At midnight 'B' Company, along with the rest of the battalion, clambered over the parapet and crawled silently to the jumping off tape just beyond the front line trench. Artillery shells continued to screech overhead and to the battalion, who had experienced light to moderate shelling at Gallipoli, it seemed like hell on earth. These thoughts soon changed dramatically at 1228 hours when the two minute barrage began.

"Bloody hell!" came a voice from the line as shell after shell flew overhead and exploded to their front, the flames turning night into day as the ground trembled and vibrated under their bodies.

"I wouldn't want to be under that," whispered Archie.

Everyone in the attack line was terrified. Was today their last? Would they die quietly or painfully?

Clancy too was scared.

"Bugger this!" he shouted, "boys! Do your best. You new blokes don't hesitate, just get stuck in and rip in to the bastards...and remember...these 'old' buggers here will look after you, so stick close".

For a moment fear disappeared from the men as they watched the barrage roll on to the second objective.

Captain Ponsonby felt for a familiar object, his whistle, and tightened his grip on it, feeling the weight of impending fate. But tonight was not a night for brass whistles as this would alert the enemy that they were on their way. Ponsonby strained his eyes and saw the second hand of his watch ticking away with cruel precision, counting down to the harrowing moment that awaited the battalion. His hand quivered as he raised it slowly to give the signal, the anticipation hanging in the air.

"Go, go, go!" he shouted as 'B' Company and the whole of the

9th Battalion, without hesitation, quickly rose to their feet and raced towards the German trench, sprinting across the war torn landscape, their boots pounding the earth as they advanced. No fire came from the German trench, for the enemy was hunkered down, seeking cover from the fierce artillery barrage. The men of the 9th Battalion couldn't believe their luck and seized the moment, adrenaline propelling them forward as they closed the gap before finally reaching their foe.

The 9th Battalion encountered several challenges during their attack on the Old German Lines. Firstly, the damage from the heavy artillery bombardment made it difficult for them to orientate themselves, and the two parallel German trench lines were not easily distinguishable. Then, to compound the situation, beneath the trenches, deep dugouts had been constructed to provide shelter for the German soldiers, the dugouts also proving to be resistant to the allied bombardment. From these positions, the German troops were poised to emerge and confront the Australian forces. Adding to the challenge, the Germans had the advantage of concealed machine guns and fortified positions surrounding the Pozières windmill. This formidable defensive setup enabled the Germans to sustain their fire on the Australian troops striving to secure the eastern flank of Pozières.

Stunned by the presence of the Aussies, as they dropped unexpectedly in to their trench, the German soldiers quickly came to their senses and charged the few paces towards their unwelcome guests. But the mud was a friend to no one as the Germans stumbled in the slippery trench, whilst the Aussies dashed and slid forward, screaming a blood curdling cry, the fury inside each man becoming a crimson rage. Captain Ponsonby swung his fist at a man recovering from a momentary stumble, his war cry rising to a loud shriek of victory as he side swiped the man's face with the muzzle and barrel of his revolver, dislodging his enemy's helmet and knocking the man to the ground; following through with a single shot to the head. Blood washed on to the floor of the trench as he raised his revolver and fired aimed shots in to any enemy soldier within killing distance. At this moment he knew nothing but the joy of battle, the pent up anger and madness for blood. Each man felt the same anger and blood lust as the ANZACs moved along the trench dealing out death at every opportunity. The Germans now seemed to be floundering, and the Aussies knew it. The slaughter was furious, bayonets swinging in the darkness finding their mark, blood and guts spurting and falling in to the mud, and the screams of men as feral as a wild Dingo's howls in the darkness.

There was a moment when the defenders were reinforced by soldiers who had suddenly appeared from dugouts to the side, and 'B' Company was slowly being forced backwards, as much by their enemy's weight as by their bayonets, which stabbed desperately in to the darkness. Clancy took hold of the lid of a wooden crate and held it like a shield, whilst gripping the stock of his rifle like a spear, growling, as he prodded the enemy with his bayonet; whilst out of immediate reach, a German soldier jabbed repeatedly at him, ducking and dodging, managing to stab low, slashing open his puttee clad right shin.

"You bastard Fritz!" Clancy yelped, but soon the burning sting of the wound was forgotten, as he crashed through the wall of the enemy like a runaway train, ramming his bayonet in to the belly of his would be killer, spilling his innards on to the earth; stealing the man's soul.

The onslaught from the raging Australians was becoming fiercer by the second, and the Germans soon broke and ran for their lives.

"Look! They're running! Let's finish 'em!" one man shouted, but acting quick to prevent a forward stampede in to the unknown, Captain Ponsonby called out for the men to hold their ground.

"Stand fast boys!" he shouted, "We *have* what we came for".

"All round defence now!" Clancy yelled out, "and try and get a breather if you can".

As the soldiers rested rifles on the parapet, staring out in to the night, water bottle corks popped as the men took a well earned gulp of water to moisten the dryness in their mouths.

Clancy slumped back on to a firing step and ran his hand down his lower right leg.

"Are you right mate?" Roo asked, as he noticed his friend wincing as he squeezed his shin.

"Those blokes must *really* sharpen their bayonets well, look, he's sliced through my bloody puttee," replied Clancy.

As Clancy squeezed his leg, his khaki puttee was dark to the eye, soaked with blood, which oozed between Clancy's fingers.

"I think it's a bit more serious than that Clance," Roo responded, "can you walk?"

"Yeah mate. I'll be right, but I think my right boot is full of blood," replied Clancy as he nodded as if to indicate that all was fine.

The Pozieres trench was taken immediately, apart from a few

strong points in OG1 and 2, although, to the attackers, time had almost stood still. Enemy fire from these trenches was heavy, so the Aussie attackers fanned out in two lines. Captain Ponsonby and Lieutenant Monteath took joint charge of the attack on OG1 and quickly moved towards the intersection with OG1, Munster Alley and Pozieres trench. The trenches were empty. The Aussies were confused but very wary.

"It must be a trick," shouted Stowie, "everyone get down".

As Stowie frantically waved and shouted at his comrades, a German machine gun opened up on them with its unmistakable brrrrrr sound, as round after round buried themselves into the parapet. The battalion safely under cover, there now ensued a bombing fight. The much lighter German egg bombs were flying over fast and furious, exploding amongst the Australian soldiers.

As Clancy tightened his puttee in order to stem the bleeding, he was annoyed.

"These Mills bombs are good, but they're too heavy to throw a great distance," he growled.

"Too bloody right they are, sir," replied a furious Private Leak, "whose game?"

Before anyone could respond, Leak was out of the trench.

"Bloody hell!" exclaimed Archie as he and Clancy glanced over to each other then instinctively followed Leak out in to no man's land.

As they ran, zig zagging through the hail of machine gun fire which was sweeping the area, all three men were hurling Mills bombs and firing their rifles from the hip. Leak, easily distinguishable as he always wore his slouch hat in to battle, continued running at the enemy post managing to score three direct hits with his bombs. Not being content with that, Archie and Clancy watched in amazement as he leapt into the enemy trench and bayoneted three unwounded Germans in quick succession. As Clancy and Archie joined him in the trench they found him surrounded by dead Germans, and calmly wiping the blood from his bayonet with his hat.

Leak looked up at his two comrades.

"My hat's buggered now. I'll never get this blood out," he said.

Archie and Clancy looked at each other in disbelief, feeling a little déjà vu from Courtney's Post.

"This looks familiar," said Archie.

Clancy turned to Leak.

"Hey Leaky, you haven't got a relative called Bert Jacka have yer?" he asked.

Leak made no reply and began to wring out the blood from his hat.

The machine gun threat was now gone so the small group cautiously made their way back to company lines.

It was now 0059 hours but there was no rest for anyone; not even the wicked. The battle was raging on all flanks. The strong point in OG1 was found to be a deep concrete lined dugout, but it was now severely damaged by the artillery bombardment, yet still a viable structure below ground.

The men of the 9th were mostly impressed by this formidable bunker built to shelter the troops during artillery attacks in order that they could resurface unscathed, and scythe down any attackers with a totally unexpected barrage of rifle and machine gun fire.

"You've got to admire Fritz eh? This must have taken months to build," Archie noted.

"Yes, it's not surprising that this line has been a stalemate for so long," agreed Captain Ponsonby.

To the right, at OG2, the battle raged on, whilst 'B' Company took up a defensive position in the captured trench.

Lieutenants Ramkena and Armstrong led the attack on OG2, but there was no sign of the trench, just churned up earth and rocks. They thus returned to the 9th Battalion positions.

With the destruction and levelling of the ground on and around the second objective, the enemy second line, there was much confusion with part of the attack group losing their bearings and ending up on the right flank of the 11th Battalion. Lieutenant White did, however, succeed in reaching and holding the objective.

Other groups from the 9th and 11th had become a little too keen and gave chase to around thirty Germans who were retreating back towards the village, pursuing them relentlessly, gradually seizing control of Pozières as they progressed through the devastated structures. The one hundred and forty Australians ignored shouts from their officers and NCOs and ran through the allied barrage, not stopping until they had reached the windmill on the far side of the Albert-Bapaume Road. On their journey they managed to catch up with and kill most of the fleeing Germans, only to find themselves on the receiving end of a friendly artillery barrage. As there were no more Germans in sight they decided to run the gauntlet of the incoming shells and make their way back to the original objective.

The second objective, including an enemy battery of 5.9 inch howitzers, was captured by 0115 hours.

At 0130 hours the 9th Battalion were now brigade reserve and held the newly captured 1st and 2nd objectives. Objective 3 was a job for another battalion and was soon taken whilst the majority of the 9th now occupied Pozieres trench.

Lieutenant White's men, for lack of a trench in which to shelter, advanced forwards, digging themselves in at the front line on the east side of the village, just south of the railway line. A platoon from the 12th joined them on their right flank making the line curve towards Pozieres trench. So the forward line was now slightly further forward than intended.

As Clancy and the OC toured the company line, along with an ammunition party, they shook hands with their men, gently patting them on their shoulders as they passed. Both men were highly thought of by the troops, not only for being soldiers of the highest calibre, but as being mates, as well as leaders. If the men needed help, advice or just re-assurance, it was always at hand; day or night.

"G'day Clance, how's your leg?" enquired Roo.

"Pretty good thanks mate. I got one of those stretcher bearer fellas to have a look. He cleaned it out and stitched it up…look…I'm right as rain again," replied Clancy as he pointed to his shin.

The men had now been on the go for well over twenty four hours and there didn't seem any time at all for any respite. But though still on the offensive, the battalion was now in reserve, manning the defensive line which had been bravely won with their blood, and here they would watch and wait whilst other battalions on both flanks passed through their new front line to press the attack yet even further forward.

As the ammunition party distributed yet more bandoliers of .303 rounds, one soldier piped up.

"Sir, my working parts are caked in carbon. If I don't get it cleaned now my weapon will be useless".

"Yes, that *is* a worrying thought," replied Captain Ponsonby as he turned to the CSM, "Clancy can we organise some sort of rota for weapon cleaning which doesn't compromise the line?"

"No worries sir," replied the CSM as he sent a whispered message down the line for all section commanders to converge on him now.

As soon as the corporals arrived a plan was put into place for every fourth man to be cleaning their rifle "as fast as lightning" as the CSM had put it, "but without scrimping on the effort". Very soon rifle butts were unscrewed and the cleaning kits removed from their housing beneath the brass butt plate. Each man then laid out his folded blanket on the muddy trench floor then began the process of removing the working parts from the breach and laying them carefully on the clean, dry blankets. Rifle sights were scrubbed clean with the wire brush, as were the bolt assemblies, then the breach itself was swept clean and dusted out with the brush. Next the cleaning cloth was fed through the eye of the metal pull through, the metal weight on the pull through cord dropped down the barrel and the cleaning cloth end pulled through to the breach. A quick visual inspection down the barrel would reveal a shining rifled inside. Lastly all working parts would be oiled, as well as the rails on which the parts sat, and the weapon reassembled. Depending on the dirtiness of the weapon, the task would be completed in five to ten minutes. The final job was to re-charge empty magazines. Working to the rota, the whole company was done in less than two hours. In the mean time the line was manned, cooking stoves were on the go and some even managed a quick nap.

Organised they may have been, but the Germans certainly had not been sitting back and twiddling their thumbs. Just ahead of the battalion line was a damaged brick wall, the perfect spot amongst the rubble for a nest of snipers. It wasn't until the first shot rang out that the Aussies were aware of their deadly foe, with Major Young and Lieutenants Wittkopp and Lukin being wounded, and Lieutenant Aggett being killed. Others too were narrowly escaping death or injury with sniper rounds cracking and whipping through the air, tossing up dirt and rocks from the parapet. Pretty soon the 9th Battalion had had enough, but it took one Sergeant Archie Taylor and his small band of men to change the status quo.

The sniper attacks had begun in the darkness, their targets being revealed to them by the occasional flare and constant flash of flame and fire as an artillery round slammed home. The snipers, themselves, seemed invisible, but with his keen eye, Archie quickly spotted the tell tale muzzle flash as the sniper's rifles sent death in their direction.

"Got yer, yer bastard!" Archie whispered to himself.

"Did you *see* that Arch?" asked Stowie.

"I did mate," Archie replied, as he glanced over to his attack party, which consisted of Stowie, Taff, Jacko and John Leak, "righto boys, slow and steady, let's be off".

Stealthily the five soldiers pulled themselves on to the top of the parapet, ensuring that they lay flat on the rim so as not to expose their silhouettes. Once they were all on the top edge of the trench Archie gave the signal to move out in to no man's land. At first the five crawled uneasily along the stony ground but soon found themselves in the remnants of a trench, meaning that they were out of sight of the enemy. Using the dead ground they stood, albeit hunched over, slowly edging their way towards the brick wall. It was evident that the snipers had not noticed them, for they continued with their sporadic sniping in all directions, whilst unknowingly guiding their soon to be assassins to their hiding place, with each flash from their rifle muzzles. In an instant the raiding party was upon them. Archie leapt on to the top of the wall, rifle slung over his shoulder, hands loaded with Mills bombs, and began lobbing his deadly cargo in all directions, whilst the rest of the men fired round after round over and around the brick barricade. The attack was over in seconds, with Archie and his group quickly pouncing on each lifeless German with a swift kick between their legs, just to confirm that they *were* dead and not putting on an act. The Aussies quickly searched each body for maps and other intelligence then began their short journey back to the Pozieres trench.

As with all patrols, they had arranged a password so as to avoid being shot by their own side. Theirs was "whisky". As they approached the front line trench a very nervous fair dinkum threw a Mills bomb without first challenging. Luckily Stowie heard the thud of the bomb hitting the ground and immediately shouted.

"BOMB! GET DOWN!"

As the patrol hugged the ground, the bomb detonated,

showering shrapnel in a conical direction up and over where the patrol now lay, missing everyone.

Archie was *not* happy and his sudden yell of "WHISKY! YOU BASTARD! WHISKY!" could be heard a mile away.

"Language dear boy," laughed Captain Ponsonby as Archie and the men jumped back in to the trench.

"Language!? Where *is* the idiot? He's going to feel my bloody fist in a minute!" Archie growled.

"Calm down sergeant, this is unlike you," said Ponsonby reassuringly.

"Sorry mate," replied Archie as he glanced along and shouted down the trench, "BUT I HAVEN'T COME ALL THIS WAY TO GET KNOCKED BY SOME JUMPY ARSE HOLE!"

Everyone within earshot heard Archie's outburst, and no-one said a word.

"Come on Archie, and the rest of you, you did a smashing job, now come and let an officer make you all a nice cup of tea," said the captain.

Archie came back to earth.

"That'll be a first," he joked.

Although the 9th held Pozieres trench, fighting was still going on to their right in OG1. Eventually artillery was called in and the enemy was pushed back to a second strong point further along the trench.

From 0130 hours on the 23rd, until daybreak, the 10th Battalion from South Australia re-enforced the 9th and gallantly fought their way in to OG1 and occupied the captured portion.

Once dawn had broken there was more enemy sniping from the ruins to the battalion's front. The artillery bombardment had ceased, so the way was clear for the Aussies to clear out the new batch of snipers. Again small parties were sent out to scour the ruined buildings, shell holes and dugouts. On seeing the advancing search and destroy parties the German snipers weren't feeling so brave this time so sought out bunkers and holes in which to hide, but the ANZACs were prepared for this and carried 'P' Bombs, or phosphorous grenades, especially useful for clearing out these rat nests.

Roo was leading one of the groups as they came upon a suspected hidey hole. No man said a word as Roo gestured with his hands the actions of pulling the pin from a grenade and pointed to the suspected hiding place.

Private Leak acknowledged Roo with a nod, reached into his satchel and produced a 'P' Bomb. Roo nodded his approval as Leak pulled the pin and tossed the bomb down in to the hole. The Aussies each threw themselves to the ground as the bomb exploded. The explosion was followed by screams and curses, in German, as the hole filled with smoke and flame and enemy soldiers, some on fire, ran from the hole shouting "nicht scheezen!" whilst the Aussies dropped each man with a hail of rifle fire.

"I wonder what they were saying?" uttered one soldier.

"Buggered if I know mate," replied Roo, "it was hard enough understanding Abdul, let alone old Fritz here".

Again the Aussies had succeeded in eliminating the snipers, but again there would be no rest for anyone. At about 0530 hours, about an hour after the sunrise, hundreds of German soldiers ran head on at the line held by the 9th and 12th Battalions.

"STAND TO!" echoed all over the Aussie front line as rifles and a lone Lewis Gun opened up on the advancing Germans.

"These Huns are as bonkers as the Turks," Stowie shouted to Clancy.

"They are mate," replied Clancy as he aimed, fired and pulled back his bolt and rammed it home again, shouting, "RIP IN TO THEM BOYS!"

The air was an orchestra of cracks, bangs and rat tat tats, as the ANZACs poured round after round into the German soldiers. Unlike the Turks who were led by their unyielding faith in Allah and promises of paradise, Fritz was not that easily swayed, with self preservation and the will to survive being their priority. As the barrage of bullets smashed into the advancing enemy, most dived for the safety of the shell holes which littered the ground like a moonscape, while others were cut in half by the accurate rifle fire of the 9th and 12th, their entrails exploding in all directions as they fell like rag dolls on to the crimson gore that was no man's land.

Clancy took a quick and guarded look above the parapet and, as the mist and fog of war slowly subsided, he couldn't see a live enemy soldier anywhere.

"CEASE FIRE! RELOAD AND BE READY!" he shouted left and right.

No sooner had he spoken than the Germans rose up again but this time began running back towards Pozieres, retreating towards the cemetery located at the northern periphery of the village.

"GIVE IT TO THEM...FIRE!" shouted Clancy.

No one felt good about shooting men in the back, but the

fact was that they hadn't surrendered and would be back, and for any doubters Clancy walked along the trench shouting "GET THEM NOW OR THEY *WILL* BE BACK!"

The Gallipoli veterans were fully aware that they needed to kill *all* enemy soldiers, so happily ripped into the fleeing Germans. The new blokes may or may not have thought about the rights and wrongs of it, but this was war and there was no room for personal thoughts, opinions or ideologies, and soon the whole 'choir' was singing, with Germans falling left, right and centre.

At the end of the fight, the ground to the battalions' front was littered with the dead and wounded, whose bodies writhed in the mud, some screaming in agony and others attempting to crawl back to the safety of their lines. The Australians let them go, drawing the line at killing a man who was already down.

The Aussies ceased firing and began reloading weapons. Some of the men clutched crucifixes which hung around their necks, others dampened their dry throats with sips from their canteens, whilst some just sank back to the floor of the trench for a brief respite.

"We're for it now boys," announced Jacko.

"What do you mean?" asked Ten Bob.

"We aint been shelled for a while, so I reckon its coming soon," replied Jacko.

"What, an eye for an eye and that sort of stuff?" asked the now concerned Ten Bob.

"Bloody oath mate," replied a stern faced Jacko.

Clancy had been in earshot of Jacko's revelation.

"Well aren't you the life and soul of the party Jacko?" Clancy remarked, "remind me not to invite you to any dos".

"I was just saying sir," said Jacko.

Clancy shook his head but knew that Jacko was probably correct.

"You're probably right mate," said Clancy, "everyone, pass it on to try and create some overhead cover of sorts...just in case".

"What are you waiting for?" yelled Corporal Stowe, "get your entrenching tools out and let's make some dugouts...tout de suite".

Jacko's prediction came true, for within an hour German shelling re-commenced, with the troops having to endure a heavy bombardment for most of the day. To the men it was the most awful din, and it seemed as though everything from hell had broken loose to taunt them. Shells were falling like summer rain.

"You know," said Archie to Roo and Clancy, "people have often told me in the course of conversations that it was raining shells, and I admit that I took it with a pinch of salt, thinking that it couldn't be possible, but look at this, it's actually really happening".

Despite the shelling, the men carried on reinforcing the trenches and their overhead cover. Meanwhile no man's land which separated the Aussies from the Germans was a tangled dump, being transformed from an already muddy mess to one great mass of craters, varying in diameter from ten to twelve yards across.

"Oh well, I suppose on the good side of things it will be hard for any Huns to come at us across that lot now," Clancy noted, but as he spoke a shell fell only three yards from where he and the Taylor boys were standing, the force of the concussion pitching the three men several yards to their left, each one landing heavily, bruised a little but not badly injured; although Roo did manage to become partly buried as a section of the trench wall collapsed on him, Clancy and Archie rapidly digging him out and pulling him free.

As Archie and Clancy helped Roo brush himself off, the three men thanked their lucky stars that it hadn't been a direct hit, knowing only too well that on occasion the Germans *did* manage to land a big howitzer shell into the Aussie trenches, adding a few more names to the death roll. Even as they stood they were showered with shrapnel which bounced and rattled off their steel helmets like marbles. Again they were unhurt, as the shell had exploded fairly high in the air, and by the time the metal balls had reached them they were spent and had no momentum, having first hit the trench parapet.

"WHAT ELSE DID YOU GET FOR CHRISTMAS YOU HUN BASTARDS?!" one soldier shouted through the din.

Once the shelling had petered out, later on in the day, the exhausted and shell weary men of the 9th were employed in digging a sap forward of the line, which then turned left and right parallel with their trench, and fronting OG1. This was to be a jumping off trench for the latest attack on OG2.

As day broke on the 24th of July, the 9th Battalion was a shadow of its former self, and as what was left of the 9th *and* 10th were to be involved in this latest venture, much needed support was required to bolster their ever dwindling numbers. This support came in the form of part of the 7th Battalion and all of the 5th Battalion from the 2nd Brigade.

Once Captain Ponsonby had held his 'O' Group, and the NCOs had departed to brief their men, Clancy voiced his concern.

"Freddy mate, the boys are stuffed. Two days on the go now," said Clancy, "and they haven't even managed to finish the jumping off trench yet either".

"I'm sorry old friend, but we're all in the same boat…and that trench *needs* to be completed before the attack tomorrow," replied Ponsonby.

"I'm beginning to think that politician bloke was right and will get his wish," said Clancy.

"Politician?" replied Ponsonby, not really sure what Clancy was talking about.

"That bloke before the war…you know…Australia will fight 'to our last man'…or something like that," said Clancy.

"Oh…that was Andrew Fisher. He's our Prime Minister now," replied Ponsonby.

"Really? Well I never…and I voted for him too," replied Clancy, "bloody typical though eh?" said Clancy.

"Typical?" asked Ponsonby.

"Yeah…I don't see him anywhere in the ranks do you…bastard politicians! They start the wars and sit back while silly buggers like us fight them!" exclaimed Clancy.

The plan this time was a full frontal assault on the enemy held positions of OGs 1 and 2, and not along the corridors of the old trenches as previously. At 0200 hours on the morning of the 25th of July the allied artillery carried out a quick yet deadly bombardment of the enemy trenches. The night was torn apart by the deafening roar of artillery fire, as shells whistled through the air before erupting in violent explosions upon impact, the ground shaking with each detonation, sending plumes of dirt and debris skyward, while the sky flashed intermittently with the bursts of light from the explosions. The barrage was intense and precise, designed to inflict maximum damage in a short span of time, creating chaos and confusion within the enemy lines.

As Stowie, awoken from his brief nap, stared at the light show, he was not a happy man.

"Can't a fella get even just an ounce of sleep round here?!"

The job of the 9th, in the first instance, was to support the assault wave, consisting of the 5th and 7th Battalions, as they attacked. The exhausted 9th, although relieved to a man, were nonetheless eager to get in to the fray.

As the attackers made their way to the jumping off trench, the men of the 9th whispered good luck to them.

One of the attack party turned to the 9th and joked "hey, the 9th, remember, shoot the Germans, not the Aussies".

This was met with a jovial response of "we'll try our best, but sometimes our best isn't always good enough".

The attack went well, with OG1 being easily taken, and OG2 finally falling at 0300 hours, after stubborn resistance. Simultaneously the far right of the 9th and 10th's position became a struggle in itself, with 'B' Company happening to occupy that zone.

There were still two strong points between OG1 and 2 which had to be taken, and a terrific bomb battle took place, lasting three hours, and resulting in heavy casualties on both sides, *and* a to and froing of ownership of the strong points. Even soldiers from the 5th, 7th and 8th Battalions lent a hand.

Bombs were flying from both directions, but the Germans seemed to have an endless supply.

As Clancy pulled the pin and tossed his grenade he looked over to his mates.

"Remind you of anything?" he asked, with a wry smile.

"Now let me think...Saturday night at the pub?" joked Archie.

"At this rate we'll soon be out of bombs," said a concerned Stowie.

"Don't worry mate I've got a few of those hard tack biscuits left; they should cause a bit of damage," joked Clancy, causing laughter amongst the men.

Luckily for 'B' Company there were a couple of 'angels of the bombs' in the guise of Lance Corporals Larsson and Swayn, and their party, who were doing their best to get ammunition and bombs up to the front line in quick time; even though exhausted themselves.

Roo noticed the supply group arrive with their previous, and much needed, cargo.

"Hey, hey...if it isn't my favourite corporals," said Roo, as he shook both men's hands firmly, whilst acknowledging the other men with a nod of the head.

Larsson and Swayn were glad to be of assistance and quickly began organising their men to distribute the bombs along the trench.

"How far *is* Fritz Roo?" Larsson asked.

"Oh, about ten or fifteen yards maybe," Roo replied.

"Ripper!" exclaimed Larsson as both men, although fatigued, began lobbing bombs towards the enemy.

Roo was pleased, calling out "Ha! Ha! The more the merrier boys!"

Passing the bombs along Pozieres Trench was not an easy undertaking, especially now that the tunnel between it and OG1 had become impassable.

Captain Ponsonby could immediately see that getting the grenades to where they were needed was a matter of life and death...theirs!

"Fellas," he called out to all within hearing distance, "I am sorry to ask, but I need a volunteer, or two, to run between us and OG1 to deliver bombs. It's dangerous I know, but our friends need our help".

"Dangerous?" Stowie piped up, "I think all of these bombs and shells flying about are just a *little* bit dangerous too...but, yeah I'll do it".

Corporal Slaughter was another keen volunteer, and probably aptly named for the job.

Both men quickly discussed what they were about to do.

"Stowie, I reckon we should lift the crates up on to the parapet, climb out, grab a box each and run like hell. What do you reckon?" asked Slaughter.

"Sounds like a good idea to me. Let's do it," replied Stowie.

The two NCOs quickly threw the boxes of bombs over the parapet, whilst all around them bombs were exploding, bullets were whizzing, and their mates were getting hit.

Both men looked at each other, breathed in deep, and were over in to no man's land. At first the Germans didn't notice them as they moved forward and backward between the two trenches, delivering messages of death to their grateful comrades. But, after fifteen minutes their ferrying operation had come to the attention of a few of the enemy, who now sprayed the area with machine gun and rifle fire, hoping to end the enterprise unfolding before their eyes.

As the two soldiers dodged left and right back to Pozieres Trench, Corporal Slaughter was clipped by a single round which bowled him over on to the muddy terrain.

Stowie was oblivious to Slaughter's plight, as it had happened to his rear, and jumped like a terrified cat, landing safely back in the company trench.

Laughing to himself at his lucky escape, he stood up and brushed himself off.

"That was close eh mate?" he shouted out to Corporal Slaughter; but there was no response.

He quickly spun around searching for his mate, but he was nowhere to be seen.

"He got knocked mate," announced Roo, pointing, "a few yards back there".

"No!" Stowie shouted, raising his head above the parapet, scanning the darkness for the fallen corporal.

Then, in the flickering light of a descending flare he spotted Slaughter, about ten yards out, still alive, and trying to drag himself towards the trench. Without hesitation, Stowie pulled himself on to the sandbagged parapet and lay flat for a while trying to work out the fall of enemy rounds. Now that he and Slaughter were no longer targets, enemy fire was again concentrated on

OG1. Seeing his chance he ran the short distance to the fallen corporal.

"Are you hurt bad?" he asked the wounded man.

"Yeah mate, I don't think I can walk…sorry," replied Slaughter.

"Nothing to be sorry about. This is going to hurt, but I am going to put you over my shoulder and carry you back," replied Stowie.

Try as he may he could not lift the wounded man. Whether it was plain exhaustion or something to do with his own wound received at Gallipoli, he did not know.

"Bugger this," Stowie grumbled as he grasped Slaughter's belt and webbing straps and managed to lift him approximately three feet off the ground. Pleased with himself he began to run the short distance with the wounded Corporal Slaughter and gently passed him down to waiting hands in the company trench. As he dropped down to safety a familiar voice rang out.

"Good one Stowie. I couldn't have done it better myself," said Clancy, a smile beaming across his face, "you're still a fat bastard but!"

Stowie smiled at his Gallipoli rescuer.

"Cheers mate," he replied, "it aint as easy as it looks".

As both men shook hands, chaos erupted around OG1 as the Germans launched a counterattack.

"Bloody hell, here we go again!" exclaimed Clancy as he glanced over at Corporal Slaughter, "stretcher bearers can you get this bloke to safety? Everyone else, hop to it and drop these bastards to our front!"

As flares suddenly illuminated the battlefield, the Aussies in OG1 and the company trench instantly sprang into action, and, along with the rest of the company, Stowie and Clancy quickly lent on the parapet and began firing at the oncoming Germans, who were moving forward in stages, some lying prone and firing whilst others advanced a few yards, themselves then lying prone and firing whilst the men to their rear moved forward.

Clancy noticed the manoeuvre and was impressed, and as he paused briefly to recharge his magazine he spoke briefly to Stowie.

"Hey mate, can you see that? They're leap frogging forward," he said, "we'll have to try that ourselves; seems to work a treat".

"Gosh Clance, only a CSM could be thinking of new tactics in a situation like this!" replied Stowie as he continued firing at the enemy soldiers.

Volleys of rifle fire cracked through the air as the ANZAC soldiers continued to fire back with expert precision, each shot slicing through the advancing enemy ranks. The Lewis Gun too was doing its job as it scythed in to the advancing German infantry, relentlessly mowing down waves of enemy soldiers, whilst some men hurled Mills bombs into the fray, the explosions sending shrapnel and bodies flying in all directions. Despite the ferocity of the attack, in true Gallipoli style, 'B' Company held their ground with their usual steely resolve and soon beat off the assault, the battlefield littered with the remnants of the enemy's failed attempt.

The 9th Battalion had managed to hold their part of the line during the 24th and 25th of July, but fighting was not their only task, with much digging and improvement of the trench system being undertaken. Stretcher bearers did some amazing work in the face of the enemy, retrieving their fallen comrades under fire. Even one of the padres had acquired a wheeled stretcher and did his bit too, rescuing the wounded. Signallers had been employed in laying and repairing communication lines, whilst battalion and brigade runners ran the gauntlet over the shell swept battlefield delivering vital messages and orders. Whether it be the carrying of ammunition and water to the front line, each man had done his part, and the Aussie war machine was well and truly oiled.

Good news came on the 26th when, at 0400 hours, the battalion was relieved. After four days of non stop fighting and digging in, with constant artillery bombardments, often with no sleep and little rest, the battalion formed up and made its way out of the line.

Although thoroughly exhausted, as they marched towards Albert, they even managed a chorus of 'Waltzing Matilda'.

The battle for Pozieres was over, for the 9th Battalion at least. It had gone into action one thousand and sixteen strong and was now reduced to six hundred and twenty three. Fifty seven men were dead, never to see Australia again or to hold their loved ones in their arms, two hundred and seventy one were wounded and sixty five were missing.

Although the remaining parts of Pozières had succumbed to the chaos, in retaliation, the Germans intensified their artillery assault on the Australian forces, relentlessly bombarding the village and its narrow approaches. By the 27th of July, the Australian 2nd Division had gained control of Pozières village and was tasked with seizing Pozières heights. The assault commenced at

0015 hours on the 29th, only to encounter formidable German defences, resulting in a failed attack and the loss of three thousand five hundred Australian soldiers. In the face of adversity, Major General James Legge, commanding the 2nd Division, proposed another assault rather than withdrawal, and following an extensive artillery barrage on the 4th of August, the Australians managed to secure Pozières heights.

At Albert the battalion received an issue of rum, and was served a hot meal. There was also a huge amount of mail to be distributed. Though some eagerly opened their letters, hoping for some normality after the past few days, most, completely done in, slept for the rest of the morning

Despite the tiredness of the men, the war had not ceased and that afternoon the battalion marched out to Warloy, fifteen miles north east of Amiens. There was much excited chatter and laughter as the men marched, no doubt brought on by a feeling of relief. Most were armed with at least one souvenir, whether it be a prized Luger, spiked helmet, a pair of jack boots, or a bottle of schnapps, each man was proud of their haul, and even prouder of what they had achieved.

"Hey, Jacko, look at this beauty!" Taff exclaimed, holding up a shiny Luger, "found it on a dead German officer the other day".

"Not bad, mate!" Jacko replied, grinning, as he pointed to the spiked helmet he had tied to his pack, "but take a gander at this...what do you reckon?"

"Yeah, not bad, Archie's got one of those too, but I don't think it would suit you though," Taff joked.

"Less of the chatter you beasties," came a voice from the ranks, "you're supposed to be marching".

It was big Sergeant MacDonald.

"Sorry Mac, I was just showing Taff my German helmet," replied Jacko.

"Oh aye wee man?" said Mac, "that spike would be a useful tool to encourage wee fellas up gang planks do you not think young Jackson".

"You're never gonna let me forget that are you Mac?" asked Jacko.

"Er...let me think," replied Mac, "No".

As all in earshot burst in to laughter, the battalion marched on.

From Warloy the battalion continued on to Berteaucourt, via La Vicogne, arriving there at 1600 hours on the 29th. The men were now very weary and appeared to all who saw them, drawn and haggard, dazed so much that they were sleep walking. But they *had* just been through hell and come out the other side! To assist the men, all of their kit was transported on wagons, nevertheless the troops were still footsore, their feet blistered and bleeding; but they marched on, being cheered at their destination by their sister battalion, the 49th, whose band had quickly assembled to play them into the village.

Two days later the battalion's mood was uplifted somewhat by the Brigadier who thanked them and complimented them for their actions in taking Pozieres, telling them that no other troops in the world could have done better. On the same day one hundred and eighty eight reinforcements arrived to bolster their diminished ranks, with another forty arriving the next day.

During their eleven days at Berteaucourt their time was occupied with training and reorganisation. The battalion Lewis Gun section was divided up into detachments, each with two guns, one detachment going to each company. Mills bombs were being adapted and improved, with a new version now being able to be fired from rifles; thus sixteen men were detailed as rifle grenadiers and attached to Battalion Headquarters. The troops were impressed with this latest development as this would resolve the range issue when delivering bombs to the enemy.

6

Pluck, dash and endurance

July was a month of twice weekly patrols for the 2nd Light Horse Regiment, with intelligence reports suggesting that the Turks and their German allies intended to attack Romani in force in order to clear a path to the Suez Canal. Thus there was no rest for the troops who, on their odd days in camp, were employed strengthening the positions at Romani, and constructing a redoubt, or place of retreat, on Katib Ganit, a high dune near Quatia Oasis. The ever shifting sand, however, made this an almost impossible task, and the works had to be manned twenty four hours a day.

In the desert the Turks were a skilful adversary, and by mid July there was no doubting his intentions, having pushed forward and strengthened positions as he went.

On the 20th of July there was news.

"Hey boys," announced Percy, "I've got some bad news. There's been a bit of a to do with Abdul, and young Gibbo from 'A' Squadron has been killed".

Chugger, Davo and Boggy were stunned, for although death is one of the inevitabilities of war, it is not something you would wish on anyone.

Chugger cleared his throat then asked what had happened.

"Oh mate; the squadron were out patrolling near some place called Oghratina when they had a contact with the Turks. They deployed for a better look but Abdul opened up quite heavy on them. Gibbo was hit pretty bad, but Corporal Cowley, Nash and Apelt managed to rescue him," Percy explained, "but he died in the hospital cart on the way home".

"Bloody hell, I'm really sorry, he was a good bloke," replied Chugger.

The Turks seemed to be very busy in the immediate vicinity, so Aussie patrols were stepped up. On the 3rd of August it was revealed that the Turks were expected to attack in a matter of days, resulting in the Brigade being hastily ordered to occupy a line of OPs from Katib Ganit to Mount Meredith, to a point one mile south east of Hod Enna. The 3rd Light Horse Regiment, with their left flank resting at the Romani redoubts, held from Katib Ganit to Mount Meredith, a distance of about one and a half miles, whilst the 2nd manned a line of two and a half miles from Mount Meredith to the extreme right, and the 1st Light Horse Regiment was in reserve. The brigade's task was to give warning of the Turkish attack. The ground to their front was perfectly open, with an unobstructed field of fire, which pleased the men no end. However, there was a down side. Due to the lack of sandbags and the unstable sandy terrain, no trenches were dug, or indeed were *able* to be dug.

"You'll just have to do your best and scrape out a shallow possie," said Percy.

As Percy observed the regiment's dispositions he could see that they were in a precarious spot. 'B' Squadron held the left of their line and were in contact with the 3rd Light Horse to *their* immediate left. 'A' Squadron were positioned on the right half of the line, whilst two machine guns, under Lieutenant Hackney, were located in the centre. 'C' Squadron, under Captain Stodart, were in support.

"Time for a brew boys?" asked Davo.

"Yeah...why not?" replied Percy, "we might not get another chance for a bit. You sort that Dave while the rest of you check your weapons and make sure there is no sand in them. Don't want any stoppages do we?"

Keeping in contact within the different regimental lines was a reasonably easy task, but it was the opposite when trying to relay messages between flanking posts. This was mainly due to the terrain, which consisted of undulating sand dunes with sides so steep that it was a marathon task to get round them in order to relay messages and mutually support other OPs. In all, each squadron consisted of one hundred men, meaning that the front line was stretched thin, with two hundred men manning a four thousand yard stretch.

There was a little excitement at around 2030 hours when the New Zealand Mounted Rifle Brigade, having been in enemy contact all day, passed through the 2nd Light Horse lines en route to their camp at Et Maler. The brigade made an impressive sight and was stretched out quite some distance, their rear guard passing through at 2115 hours. However, thirty five minutes later it became apparent that the Turks had been cunningly following the New Zealanders, as at 2150 hours an enemy advance guard exchanged fire with an 'A' Squadron picquet near Hod Enna.

"STAND TO!" reverberated all along the line, as 'C' Squadron, although still in support, readied themselves for the expected fray.

Within minutes the 2nd Light Horse's line came under fire from all directions along its front, with rounds buzzing around like blow flies on a summers day, as the Turks probed for weaknesses. The Turks had arrived in huge numbers and were starting to swarm, resulting in the ANZAC line being shortened and thickened so as to prevent an imminent enemy break through.

There was no whispering now, as orders were barked in every direction.

Lieutenant Righetti was suddenly on the scene and was rounding up men, calling out to Percy.

"Sergeant Taylor!"

"Sir?!" replied Percy.

"Gather up your troop and follow me," shouted the officer.

Percy quickly glanced along the line, shouting left and right.

"Come on boys, follow Mr Righetti...let's go!"

Without hesitation the men followed the officer to a gap in the line between 'B' Squadron and the machine gun position to their right, where Lieutenant Righetti directed them to their defensive line.

"Right sergeant, spread your men along this line as thinly as you can. There are no friendlies to your front, so if anything comes from that direction drop 'em," explained Righetti.

"No worries skipper," replied Percy, turning to his men, "you heard the man, anything to our front is fair game so make ready and let's get to it boys".

Urgent orders were sent to 'A' Squadron to withdraw from the line, along with the machine guns from the right, to a position to the rear of the regiment's left.

The nature of the ground made any movement in the dark very difficult. 'B' Squadron were ordered to hold on at all costs, resulting in additional ammunition being sent their way. If the enemy were to break through their defensive position the entire right of the line would be cut off.

Enemy pressure was increasing by the minute. It soon became evident to the Aussie soldiers that, in open warfare, Johnny Turk was an even better and more skilled adversary, than he had been at Gallipoli; and certainly not one to be written off. The Ottoman Empire had dominated the middle east and parts of Europe for over four hundred years, and was not about to relinquish its grip.

Field telephones were an essential means of communication on the modern battlefield, but pretty soon after the appearance of the Turks, the telephone line was cut and no further message from brigade headquarters was received for twelve hours, when some brave signaller had managed to locate and repair the break. The last message that *had* been received was at 0330 hours, when a squadron from the 1st Light Horse Regiment arrived in support.

All of 'C' Squadron was deployed on the front line by 0200 hours, but even with an increase in numbers, and the lead they were sending towards the enemy, it was obvious to the troops that they wouldn't be able to hold for very long.

"It's getting a bit hairy at a hundred yards eh sir?" Percy announced to Lieutenant Righetti.

"That it is Sergeant Taylor," he replied, as he pondered the situation then made a sudden snap decision, "Percy I think we need to prepare for the worst. Take one man, go to the rear and select a fallback position for us just in case we get overwhelmed here".

"Bloody hell sir, I knew it was bad, but not that bad," replied an astonished Percy, as he turned to one of his mates, "but better to be safe than sorry…Chugger…on me…let's go".

As Percy and Chugger moved cautiously to the rear, and mounted their horses, it appeared, from the distant gun fire and explosions, that the main attack seemed to be taking place at Mount Meredith, with the 3rd Light Horse and 'B' Squadron involved in some heavy fighting. After the moon had set at around 0230 hours, the Germans and Ottomans had launched a bayonet charge on Mount Meredith, and in the darkness, the light horsemen had to resort to aiming at the flashes of the enemy's rifles until the fighting was close enough for bayonets. Despite being vastly outnumbered, the light horsemen mounted an effective delaying action at close quarters, until they were gradually forced to relinquish ground and ultimately evacuate the position by 0300 hours.

Simultaneously, the Turks were taking advantage of the shortened defensive line and marching past the right flank towards Mount Royston.

The troops on the right of the line waited anxiously for news of 'A' Squadron's successful withdrawal, as they would act as a covering force for the other withdrawing units. Everyone felt nervous as they watched for the first glimpses of dawn, for the darkness was their friend, disguising their numbers from the overwhelming Turkish and German attackers. The 2nd Light Horse's left flank was also now exposed following the 3rd Light Horse Regiment's withdrawal of its right, after the enemy's capture of Mount Meredith at 0300 hours.

There was still no word from 'A' Squadron. Major Markwell was sent to hasten and direct the 'A' Squadron operation, but had become disorientated in the pitch black darkness. The rest of the 2nd, in order to buy Markham some time, held on.

The darkness echoed with rifle and machine gun fire as weapons of war spat death in to the black night. The Aussies were expert shots to a man and the speed in which they fired and reloaded was remarkable, almost like a human machine gun…bang…up, back, eject, forward, down, and bang again.

As Boggy and Davo fired in to the night, Boggy looked up and saw Lieutenant Righetti running up and down, helping and encouraging the men, with a complete disregard of his own danger.

"POUR IT IN TO THEM MEN!" Lieutenant Righetti

shouted along the line, as he calmly directed and spurred on his troopers.

Boggy yelled at him to get out of sight, but he was unmoved, raising his pistol to get off another shot, when a bullet went clean through his head. As he fell back a Turkish bomb exploded in the air above him, showering his lifeless body with shrapnel.

Boggy shook his head in sadness for yet another life snuffed out, then rejoined the fight, firing his weapon and tossing the occasional bomb in to the Turkish hordes.

The Turks tried all night to drive the Light Horse out, their assaults failing whenever it came to close quarter fighting. There were thousands of them, or so it seemed to the defenders, who could hear the whistles blowing behind them, and their cries of "Allah! Allah!" When the Turks got close, they would be greeted with "RAPID FIRE!!" and melt away. It was a devil of a scrap; dead and wounded everywhere, friend and foe alike.

By 0320 hours the 2nd Light Horse was surrounded on three sides, the firing line having been forced back to the horses, where Chugger and Percy waited in order to act as guides to the position they had selected.

"Over here boys, mount up, mount up," Percy yelled in the darkness.

The enemy, at this point, were a mere fifty yards distant, with some being unexpectedly closer. A number of horses had been killed, leaving their riders, in their heavy boots and leggings, to try to traverse the sandy terrain. Sadly, some of the ANZACs fell foul to the spritely, barefooted Turks, who were able to outrun the lighthorsemen and take them prisoner. But the great scamper was on for those who still had their mounts, many of whom reached out in the darkness to their horseless mates, lifting them on to the rear end of their steeds.

"There you go cobber," whispered Chugger, as he yanked a running soldier up on to his horse's rear, "we'd better make tracks quick smart eh?"

But Chugger's passenger remained quiet, the silence being broken by the sound of a pistol hammer being cocked, the cold steel of its muzzle sending a shiver down Chugger's spine as it touched the back of his neck. This action was followed by a voice in broken English.

"Prisoner," uttered the Turk, who had been inadvertently rescued by Chugger.

"Not bloody likely mate!" replied Chugger, who, realising his predicament, and not wanting to be taken prisoner, pulled hard on the reins and abruptly halted his horse, causing the Turk to lose his balance.

Chugger then helped the Turk on his way with a head butt to his rear.

"Have some of that you Abdul bastard!" he shouted as he spurred his horse into a gallop, leaving the stunned Turk lying in the sand.

It was a close run thing, but the regiment successfully escaped what could have been a slaughter, with bullets whizzing and whining past them.

Never before had the regiment turned its back on the enemy, galloping out of harm's way into the night.

"Well that was bloody novel!" Percy shouted to Chugger as his horse caught up and cantered parallel with his mate.

"Yeah. Did you see that cheeky bugger on the back of old George here?" asked Chugger.

"I did. But you showed him who was boss eh?" replied Percy, "I finished him off as I rode by with a quick slice of my bayonet".

Chugger nodded his approval.

Suddenly there was a shout in the darkness.

"SECTIONS ABOUT!...ACTION FRONT!"

The regiment had arrived at its fallback position and expertly carried out the order, turning about as a disciplined unit, to face the advancing Turks. They were quickly joined by the squadron from the 1st Light Horse which had arrived as support.

"FRONT RANK...ENEMY FRONT...ONE ROUND ONLY...VOLLEY FIRE...FIRE!"

As the wall of lead slammed in to the Turks, many fell dead, others screaming in agony, whilst those who had not been hit suddenly halted, looking uneasily round at their comrades, unsure of what to do.

"FRONT RANK RELOAD...SECOND RANK...ADVANCE!"

Like clockwork the second rank of lighthorsemen passed between the men and horses of the front rank and halted approximately ten paces to their front. Then came the order.

"SECOND RANK...ONE ROUND ONLY... VOLLEY FIRE...FIRE!"

As this new hail of .303 projectiles ripped in to the enemy, they did not run away, but simply withdrew slowly in to the darkness. Out of sight, but still there.

The order was given to form a defensive line where they stood. The men dismounted and three men from each section handed their horses to the fourth man who would lead the horses fifty yards to the rear…to safety.

"Davo!" shouted Percy.

"Yes mate?" replied Davo.

"It's your turn to take the horses. Look after yourself and we'll see you later," said Percy, as he Chugger and Boggy handed over their reins to their mate.

The loose sand was still not their friend so the troops did their best and managed to dig shallow shell scrapes.

The ridge that the 2nd now manned was held all night, despite the sniping and many probing attacks that were made by the enemy. Weapons were quickly cleaned, but not fully stripped down, every third man at a time, with sand being blown and brushed from the working parts and barrel, and oil being smeared liberally on the bolt and its runners.

"Check your magazines too boys. No point in feeding sand up your breach," said Percy.

On their first attempt the Turks crawled out of their positions, straight towards the dug in Australians. In the dim light the diggers could see them against the skyline. Percy and others passed the word along the line, and when the first of the Turks got within ten yards, the Aussies cheered and shouted, standing up and firing as fast as they could. There was no thought of cover, the men just blazed away until their rifles glowed red hot. The intensity of the fire fight was such that the sounds of gunfire and shouting filled the air, creating a chaotic symphony of battle. The smell of gunpowder and cordite was thick, and the flashes from the rifles lit up the night, the adrenaline coursing through the Australians' veins giving them the courage and stamina to hold their ground fiercely. Despite the initial surge, the Turks' morale broke under the relentless barrage, and they turned and fled, leaving the battlefield littered with spent cartridge cases, dead and wounded, and the echoes of a failed assault. The Australians, though exhausted, felt a deep sense of relief as they regrouped for the next onslaught.

"I don't know how long we can stand against these numbers," uttered Boggy, but his question was very soon answered, for in a few minutes they came again, and the same action was repeated.

There were no machine guns available, so the troops had to fire away with their rifles as quickly as they could. After the second repulse the enemy changed their tactics and came at the ANZACs from front and flank, obviously trying to get behind them.

The soldiers, realising the gravity of the situation, redoubled their efforts, their fingers working the rifle bolts with increasing speed and precision. The lack of machine guns meant that each shot had to count, and the men focused intensely on their targets, aware that their position depended on their accuracy and rapid response. The enemy's new strategy created a heightened sense of urgency among the ANZACs, as they could see the attempts to encircle them. The defenders quickly adjusted their formation, shouting commands and signalling to one another to cover the flanks and prevent the enemy from breaching their lines. This adaptation required remarkable coordination and bravery, as soldiers shifted their positions under fire, maintaining a relentless barrage to keep the enemy at bay. The atmosphere was tense as sounds of rifle fire and shouting echoed in the darkness, with every man aware that the outcome of this confrontation could determine their survival.

Despite the battle raging around them, the area to the front of 'C' Squadron suddenly became deathly quiet.

"Hey Perce," whispered Chugger, "got any Mills Bombs on yer mate?"

Percy fumbled in his satchel and tossed Chugger a bomb.

"Here you go mate".

In the dim light Chugger put his finger to his lips, then strained to hear.

"Listen...can you hear the buggers crawling?" he whispered to all in earshot.

The standard fuse timer setting on a Mills Bomb was seven seconds, but Chugger had a plan.

Quietly slipping his forefinger in to the ring of his Mills Bomb, he waited patiently, gently easing the pin from the bomb as he listened.

"Right," he whispered, "pass it along to take cover, because this is going to be close".

Clasping the bomb with both hands, he slowly pulled out the pin, whilst simultaneously holding on to the arming handle thus preventing it from flying off, and not only making a tell tale metal sound, but arming the bomb too early. Grasping the bomb, he gently eased off the arming handle. Now it was armed, and Chugger's heart was racing as he quickly counted to himself, "One, two, three, four, five," then, in and under arm motion quickly threw the bomb high and long.

"GET DOWN!" he shouted, as the bomb exploded low to

their front, showering the Turkish soldiers, who were crawling towards them, with shrapnel.

"Share that amongst you, yer bastards!" Chugger shouted triumphantly, as screams of agony echoed in the darkness.

"Bloody hell mate. That was close. I thought for a moment we were going to be wearing that one," whispered Percy.

"No fear of that mate," replied Chugger.

No sooner had the explosion subsided than a lone Turk suddenly came running towards them, screaming "Allah! Allah!" as he ran, and as he reached the Aussie line, his rifle, complete with bayonet, held above his head, Chugger rose to his feet and swiftly kicked the Turk forcefully between his legs, then followed through with a hard thump on the man's back with the butt of his rifle. As the Turk squirmed on the sandy ground, Percy quickly rammed his bayonet in to the soldier's ribs, obviously hitting the right spot as the soldier went still.

Percy and Chugger exchanged satisfied, yet regretful, glances, then, without a word, lay back down in their firing positions.

Somewhere in the darkness a nervous suggestion was uttered about retiring, and, all around, there were angry cries of "Who said retire?" Needless to say the Aussies stayed put.

The situation was awful, but every man was determined to stick to his position, and, along with the firing, they were yelling and shouting like demons.

The rising sun revealed a frontage strewn with hundreds of dead Turks.

Chugger looked at the scene and shook his head.

"Blimey, the row we made last night must have tricked the Turks into thinking there were more of us!" he exclaimed, "look, they are all round us within ten yards. If they'd have carried on forward we'd have been for it".

"Hey look over to the right!" a voice shouted from the line.

"Well, strike me handsome, its Major Birbeck and his crew," announced Chugger.

"I don't think there'll be much chance of that mate," replied Boggy.

"Huh? Chance of what?" asked Chugger.

"You becoming handsome," laughed Boggy.

"Oh, cheers mate," replied Chugger, rolling his eyes.

At last some welcome relief had arrived, as the party trudged through the heavy and ever shifting sand.

So far every position back to Et Mala near the main position at Romani had held, but pretty soon wily old Abdul had worked his way around the right and was attempting to outflank the regiment and its horses, being able to lay down enfilading fire.

As the barrage of rifle rounds kicked up the dust around them, there was nothing to be done except mount up and scamper a few hundred yards to the rear, each section turning briefly towards the enemy as they moved, to send death in their direction. As they withdrew, the regiment searched for signs of the expected infantry and artillery support. But, there was nothing.

Their old mate Bill the Bastard, a huge and obnoxious Waler, had been in the thick of it during the early hours too. After his time on Gallipoli, where he had been used a pack horse and mail carrier, Bill was back with the regiment, and had a new rider...one who could actually stay in the saddle for once; one Major Shanahan. During the Turkish attack he, and Bill, had come across four horseless soldiers who were on the verge of being surrounded by the enemy, but Shanahan made an astonishing gallop towards the oncoming Turks, and ordered the four men to climb aboard Bill. With two men sitting on Bill's rump and the other two with one foot in the two stirrups, the five men, and Bill, rode to safety, firing as they went. Major Shanahan was wounded in the leg during the rescue and this wound would put him out of active service.

Casualties during the night had been light, but still never welcome.

At around 0600 hours the 2nd Brigade arrived in support, and enemy attacks slackened off, as the main Turkish force marched across the regimental front to threaten the railway line at Romani. The Aussies could not believe the audacity of it. Percy, being one of them, searched with his eyes for a nearby officer, but they must have been away at briefings for there were none to be seen.

"MEN!" he shouted, to all in ear shot, "look to your front. Let's give these buggers a parting gift shall we?"

There were groans of agreement, as each man readied his rifle. Percy barked the order.

"ENEMY COLUMN ACROSS YOUR FRONT, ONE HUNDRED YARDS, INDEPENDENT FIRE AT WILL, CARRY ON!"

The 2nd Regiment's front line erupted in to a storm of rifle fire as Turks began to fall like tin cans on a fence. The firing lasted for a little under a minute, the soldiers managing to drop a few of the enemy and send them away with a limp.

As the firing ceased one ANZAC shouted out "See yous later Jacko!"

Various units, including a squadron of the 1st Light Horse Regiment, and part of the 3rd Light Horse, had mixed with and swelled the ranks of the 2nd, for which the men were grateful. There was an added bonus with the arrival of the 2nd Brigade; that being the withdrawal of the 1st Brigade from the line, to reform and act as Division reserve.

At noon, following a meeting between the CO and General Chauvel, the regiment was placed under Brigadier General Royston, the commander of the 2nd Brigade. This was a very welcome appointment as far as the men were concerned, for the Brigadier General, born in the colony of Natal, was a seasoned military officer with a storied past. Royston began his military career in the late 1870s as an enlisted soldier in the Natal Mounted Rifles, fighting in the Zulu War and, by the Second Boer War, he had risen through the ranks to command a contingent of Western Australian Mounted Infantry. His distinguished service continued through the Zulu Rebellion and into the Great War where his military prowess and leadership marked him as a formidable and respected figure, especially to the Aussies who did not suffer foolish leaders gladly.

The ANZACs had plenty of soldiers, but currently only part of the ANZAC Division had been in action against the enemy. This was about to change. Now that the Turks had shown their hand and had revealed their intended objectives, it was a relatively simple matter to foil their plans. The ANZACs were tired, but the Turks, who had marched rapidly during the night, *and* run in to an unexpected battle with the 1st Brigade, were also fatigued.

"I think that Jacko is buggered boys," announced Chugger.

"Well, we did give 'em what for, didn't we?" replied Davo.

The 2nd Light Horse, to a man, were extremely pleased with themselves, knowing that their strenuous defence had upset the enemy's plans by forcing him into an earlier than expected deployment.

"All we need to do now is finish the job eh boys?" said Boggy, feeling quite smug.

"Yeah, well, mind you get those weapons cleaned, and get some grub into you," said Percy, "ammo re-supply is in fifteen minutes so grab what you can".

"Grub?" asked Boggy, "are we getting a re-supply of that too? I've only got these bloody hard tack biccies".

"Sorry mate, we'll have to wait for the supply train to catch up with us. I'm sure we've got enough between us to share round," replied Percy, as he searched his pack for what few morsels he had left.

During the night of the 4th, the regiment became yet another outpost, extending the right of the 7th Light Horse's line towards Mount Royston. Thankfully, the night was uneventful, apart from a few shots and flares here and there, and it appeared that Johnny Turk was resting up for another big push. Just before dawn, the 7th and 2nd Light Horse Regiments, and the Wellington Mounted Rifles, however, had other plans, with all concerned forming a long, thin, extended line, and advancing on foot, bayonets fixed, towards Mount Meredith.

"Nothing like a nice walk at sunrise eh?" joked Chugger.

"Perhaps they've got brekkie on the go for us," laughed Percy.

"I'm sure that whatever it is, it will be hot," replied Davo, feeling somewhat apprehensive about their morning stroll.

With the lack of artillery support it was hoped that a show of force would be enough to rattle the Turks, who did not like the cold steel of the bayonet; unlike the ANZACs who seemed to relish it.

As the sun began to slowly rise over the barren, undulating landscape of the desert, the distant silhouette of the Turkish soldiers emerged against the golden hues of the rising sun, their bayonets glinting ominously. The Australian and New Zealand soldiers, their slouch hats pulled low over their brows, exchanged quick glances and tightened their grip on their rifles, then stepped off as one. There was tension, thick in the air as both sides braced for the impending clash, the Turks watching nervously as three regiments of ANZAC soldiers seemed to fill the ground to their front. As they drew closer to the Turkish lines, their stride grew more confident with every step, and with a final surge of speed, they lowered their bayonets, then, like a great sea wave breaking on the beach, a vast wave of khaki burst from their ordered line and swept the intervening one hundred yards, filling the Turkish positions.

An awful battle then commenced. Hand to hand fighting of the most desperate nature. With breathtaking bravery, they plunged headlong into the heart of the enemy formation, their bayonets flashing in the sunlight like deadly spears. Dozens fell before reaching the Turkish line, but for those who did reach it, the clash was fierce and unforgiving, a swirling melee of steel and sweat as the two forces battled ferociously.

During the fight, Percy jumped in between two Turks and bayoneted one, leaving bayonet and rifle in him. Then, to save himself he pounced on the other soldier, who was in the act of bayoneting *him*. The Turk missed, as Percy jumped, Percy managing to elbow the Turk aside and quickly free his bayonet from the other man, then swivelling round and thrusting his bayonet deep in to the Turk's belly. As the Turk grimaced, and fell, clasping the hilt of Percy's bayonet, Percy thought of how awful the sensation was when bayoneting a man, then quickly coming to the realisation that, although it was such a deadly business, you must get over it and keep going; for it is why you are a soldier, and you do it because your mates depend upon you.

The Australian and New Zealand soldiers drove back the enemy with each thrust of their bayonets, their war cries echoing across the battlefield, as they swept the main Turkish force off the top of Mount Meredith. Victory, for now, was theirs.

One thousand prisoners were taken after the battle, but the majority of the enemy soldiers were making their escape towards Katia. The Brigade horses were led up to the ANZACs in order that all mounted troops could pursue the fleeing enemy.

"Ah, Davo, good to see you mate," joked Chugger.

"Hey! Next battle you can look after the horses. It's *my* turn to wallop a few Abduls now boys," replied Davo.

As each section member took hold of their horse's reins they gratefully patted Davo on the back.

"You did a good job with the horses mate. The next Turk is

yours," said Percy, turning to Chugger, "Chug. Horses are yours next stunt".

Chugger was relieved inside, and waved his hand in acknowledgement.

"Thank God for that," he thought to himself.

In the end the horses were too exhausted for any impression to be made on the retreating Turks, and, on that same afternoon, the 2nd Light Horse Regiment was returned to the 1st Brigade.

"I'm not surprised we couldn't do much today. I mean, the horses have had no water for what, fifty two hours?" said Percy.

"And don't forget that we haven't eaten for a day; or slept for two nights," added Boggy.

"Yeah I reckon it's time for another word with the union rep eh boys?" laughed Chugger.

The regiment's casualty list for the last few days was ten dead, twenty two wounded, and eight taken prisoner, and this, combined with the lack of the bare essentials of life, and the extreme desert heat, resulted finally with the 2nd being withdrawn to Romani for a rest.

The next day was spent burying the dead and collecting abandoned enemy equipment.

"So much for a flamin' rest!" exclaimed Boggy, as he flopped down on the sand.

"I'm with you mate, *and* I'm bloody starving," moaned Chugger, "my belly is groaning so much I could have a conversation with it".

"Well you can tell your belly that its dinner time Chug," announced Percy, as he arrived complete with a large sack slung over his shoulder.

As the boys looked over the sack which Percy was holding, they noticed that it was dripping with blood. The three men glanced at each other, each one wondering whether or not he should ask. Finally Davo nudged Chugger quite hard in the ribs.

"Ow! Alright, alright!" yelped Chugger, "I'll be the mug. What's in the sack Perce?"

"Oh, just some meat," replied Percy.

"Meat?!" exclaimed a puzzled Boggy, "had a delivery from the butchers have we?"

"Don't be so bloody silly," said Percy.

Davo suddenly gulped.

"Hang on a mo. We're not eating dead Turks are we?" he asked hesitantly.

"Close...we're eating their horses and mules. There's plenty of dead ones lying around the place...and it's not as though they're not fresh is it?" announced Percy.

"I've never eaten horse before. It sounds a bit like eating your mate," said a concerned Chugger.

"I have," Boggy added.

"Really? How come?" asked a surprised Percy.

"It was back in the old country mate. We were bloody starving so we had no choice," replied Boggy.

"Bloody hell. Sorry mate," said Percy feeling guilty that he had asked.

Davo sat in contemplation.

"Righto, I'll do it. What does it taste like?" he asked.

"It's quite nice actually...a bit like beef, only sweeter," Boggy answered.

"Sweet beef eh?" said Chugger, "well? Are we waiting for an invite? Let's get a fire going".

During the clear up the boys had amassed a pile of wood from crates, barrels and even carts. Boggy sang quietly to himself as he constructed a sizeable campfire and lit it.

"Build a bonfire, build a bonfire…put the officers on top. Put the NCOs in the middle, and burn the bloody lot!"

"Charming…" laughed Percy.

Boggy looked up towards Percy and shook his head.

"No…not *you* of course sarge," he laughed, winking at the others.

"What was that tune mate? I'm sure I've heard Stowie humming it before," asked Chugger.

"Oh…erm…it's an American song, I think it's called *My Darling Clementine* or the like, but these aren't the proper words though," Boggy replied.

"It's a good song mate, and one to keep in the back pocket," said Chugger.

As the horse steak hissed and sizzled in the pot, the word, *and* aroma, soon got out, and it was horse steak all round. At last the Brigade had a good feed.

However, all good things, including rest periods, must come to an end, and although the higher command had deemed the troops too exhausted to pursue the Turks, they marched out on the 8th to attack the enemy rear guard at Bir-El-Abd, some twenty two miles away. At daybreak on the 9th they reached the enemy positions and discovered the Turkish rear guard to be dug in and well prepared and, after a bloody engagement, the lack of food and water forced a withdrawal.

This particular fight, however, nearly ended badly for one of the section.

As the regiment withdrew from the skirmish, Percy glanced back over his shoulder and saw Boggy riding wide to the left, when his horse thrust a hoof in to a deep rut in the ground. Despite his mate being about twenty yards away, Percy heard the grinding crack of breaking bone, and watched as Boggy tumbled, and his horse thrashed about as it crumpled to the ground, screaming in agony. Percy quickly turned his horse, Sandy, towards him and saw a large group of Turkish infantrymen coming fast. Quickly looking left and right, he shouted out to Davo and Chugger for assistance.

"DAVO! CHUGGER! QUICK, GIVE ME SOME COVERING FIRE".

The two mates halted their horses, unslung their rifles and obliged, firing aimed shots at the advancing Turks, whilst Percy fixed his long bayonet to his rifle and, holding it like a lance, spurred his horse on in the direction of the Turks, who were running fast towards Boggy. Dozens of the squadron had now turned with Percy and, on seeing this, many of the Turks tried to swerve and dodge out of the way, but Sandy was tearing in to the earth now, his nostrils wide and snorting, as Percy lowered his 'lance' and caught the closest Turk in the chest. Blood spurted and bubbled from the Turk as Percy's makeshift lance jerked back, causing the rifle to glide through Percy's hand until he was just able to grip it firmly at the stock. As the dying soldier fell to the ground, the rifle was dragged from Percy's grasp, leaving him defenceless. A second Turk stabbed at him with his bayonet but Percy managed to throw off the stroke with a firm kick with his right boot, whilst simultaneously turning Sandy with the pressure of his knees. Whilst this was happening Boggy had managed to pull Percy's rifle from the dead Turk and toss it back to his mate, who caught it just as a Turkish cavalryman closed in on him, flailing at him with a sword. It was not the Turk's day as Percy ripped his long blade across his throat, the man clasping his neck as he vomited blood from his mouth, while his eyes seemed to roll back in his head. Percy then leaned over, grabbed the man's reins and shouted to Boggy.

"DRAG THE BUGGER OFF AND CLIMB UP!"

Without hesitating, Boggy pulled the bleeding man from his horse and clambered in to the saddle, which was now a slippery and bloody mess. Percy then shouted to all of the troopers, who had come to assist, to withdraw quick smart.

"Hang on mate, chuck us your rifle," shouted Boggy as he circled his fallen mount and halted as close as he could. Then with a carefully aimed shot he put down his pain stricken horse.

"I couldn't leave him to those bastards," said Boggy as he wiped a tear from his eye, and tossed the rifle back to Percy.

The Turks who remained had given up their attack and withdrew to the safety of their lines, whilst Percy and Boggy spurred away. Boggy was swearing and cursing as they galloped, for the Turkish cavalryman had obviously not been very tall in stature as his stirrups were set quite high, and Boggy had to be content with holding on to the pommel of the saddle as his legs hung freely.

This was the final molestation of the enemy retreat, and although happy to have their mate back, and to be riding away from danger, the light horsemen were not pleased.

"Perce you've got to get the word to the officers mate," said Davo.

"The word?" asked a baffled Percy.

"Yeah mate," replied Davo, "they need to start using us properly. We are mobile infantry, and I reckon that if they'd used us to the full from the start not a single Turk would have got away".

Percy agreed with Davo but was also aware, and imparted such to his mates, that this was a new type of warfare and the doctrine was being written and updated after each battle.

Davo nodded.

"Yeah, I suppose you're right. You learn something new every day...right?"

The Brigade returned to Romani on the 13th of August, and were thanked by the Brigade Commander, Colonel Meredith, for all that they had accomplished.

Constant patrolling and fighting from May to August had taken its toll on men and horses and it was now time for a *real* rest.

"Gallipoli may have been noisy but at least you could get *some* sleep," noted Boggy.

For once, light duties actually occurred, much to the delight and relief of the men, who were able to relax on the evenings, catching up with letter writing and just general chit chat.

"Hey Perce, you're a clever bloke...is it true that this place is where all the Bible stories happened?" asked Chugger.

"Well, Archie is the clever one really, but, yes I think they did. In fact I am sure that Moses and the Hebrews passed this way on their forty year journey to the promised land," replied Percy.

"Forty years?!" exclaimed Chugger, "it's only a couple of

hundred miles! They must be bloody slow walkers. I've seen old swaggies get round Queensland in just a few months, and that must be twenty times bigger than this place!"

"Hey, have you heard that the officers are doing sword practice?" Boggy piped up, "I think there'll be a few horses minus their ears if you ask me".

All in earshot chuckled at the thought.

"I *have* heard through the furphy net that we are going to be learning something called shock tactics though," said Davo.

"Shock tactics?! What the blazes are they?" exclaimed Chugger.

Not knowing the answer, Davo shrugged his shoulders and just looked around all present hoping for some assistance; but none came.

Shock tactics or not, the men spent their evenings revising and learning new military subjects and were able to add to the subject matter with thoughts and ideas gleaned from their own personal experiences.

7

From shirkers to workers

On the 9th of August the 9th Battalion headed back to the line, via Bonneville, where it encamped for five days. The march to Bonneville was a short six miles. The day was very hot and the 9th, who were proud of their marching discipline, were at the head of the Brigade. This was a day where a proportion of the new recruits were proving to be lazy, unfit, and barrack room lawyers, as thirty two of them fell out and rested at the side of the road. The second in command, Major Salisbury, was unimpressed, angrily shouting "Call yourself soldiers!?..." whilst veterans fell out in an attempt to spur the men on with encouraging words, but instead ending up pushing, shoving or kicking them in to action, and even grabbing them by the webbing straps and dragging the men back in to formation. The shirkers and laggers didn't escape the eye of the new Regimental Sergeant Major, RSM Corfield who, on arrival at their destination, paraded them in front of the CO for a severe tongue lashing, then on to the Regimental Medical Officer (RMO) who passed them all as physically fit.

Now it was the RSM's turn as he fell the thirty two men in to three ranks.

"You men ought to be ashamed," he growled, "we have all heard about larrikins and trouble makers back home; but here you are. And I'm not happy!"

From the ranks came a whisper which did not go unnoticed by Corfield.

"Aint he a bastard?"

The RSM's response was immediate and unexpected.

"I *know* I'm a bastard," he retorted, "but I'm a *persistent* bastard. You men are a bloody disgrace! You're *supposed* to be volunteers, so try acting like it".

There was a silence in the ranks as, for many, the shame of their actions began to set in. All were soon awoken by the RSM's voice.

"PARTY...SHUN!"

The shocked group sprang to attention.

"SLOPE... ARMS! ABOUT...TURN! BY THE RIGHT...QUICK...MARCH!"

This was pack drill at its worst as the RSM drilled the men for two hours, doubling them here, there, and everywhere.

Of the thirty two, nine of the reluctant soldiers were members of 'B' Company.

No sooner had the RSM's drill ceased; Captain Ponsonby ordered a company parade.

"COMPANY...BRACE UP AND SHOW THE MOVEMENT...COMPANY...SHUN!" shouted CSM McBride, who then marched up to his OC, smartly halted and saluted.

"B Company on parade, and awaiting your address, sir".

Captain Ponsonby returned the CSM's salute.

"Thank you sergeant major, fall in please," replied the officer.

The CSM marched to the rear of the company, halted, and carried out a left turn. As his right foot slammed in beside his left, Captain Ponsonby paused.

"B COMPANY...STAND AT...EASE...COMPANY...SHUN!"

Captain Ponsonby began his address.

"There are nine men in this company, *and* twenty three others in the battalion, who are a bally disgrace! You know who you are, and all of *these* men present today know who you are too. This is the army. It is not a democracy. You do what you are told, and work *with* your fellow soldiers, not against them. There are no unions here so get that out of your skulls. I don't want to see a repeat of today again! Do you understand?!"

"Yes sir," came nine voices, as the remainder had no reason to answer.

"Soon we will be in battle. You need to depend on each other. You need to win. If you don't, you will die...no question. Sergeant Major, do you have anything to add?"

"Yes sir. You new blokes are replacing bloody good blokes who died doing their best. If you're not here to do *your* best you can meet me for a chat behind the barn over yonder and we'll see how much of a man you really are. Enough said?" the CSM barked.

Not surprisingly there were no takers for the CSM's 'chat', and there were no further issues with malingerers or larrikins.

Bonneville turned out to be an extremely quiet village for a large bunch of soldiers who had been recently paid, for there was not a single shop to be seen. To add to this there was only a daily ration of water, for drinking purposes, so if you wanted a wash or shave, you went thirsty. Then there was the bright idea of withdrawing the mens' blankets as the weather was now warmer.

"Bloody idiots! Don't they *think* it is cold at night?!" exclaimed Stowie.

"Good job we have our sleeping bags eh boyos?" added Taff.

The 14th of August meant yet another move for the 9th Battalion as they marched the nine miles to Herissart, but this time at least, not one man fell out. The following day the battalion moved on to Vadencourt where they bivouacked in 'Rest Wood'. It was here that General Birdwood took the opportunity to address and meet with the men, as well as to present many with the decorations they had bravely earned. Although not set in stone it was also announced that Private John Leak had been recommended for the award of the Victoria Cross for his bravery at Pozières. At that time, the VC was the most prestigious award for valour in battle that an Australian, or British Empire, soldier could receive. Upon hearing the news of his recommendation, Leak's mates were quick to voice their admiration with cheers and applause spontaneously erupting from the ranks, the respect and pride in their voices underscoring the significance of the honour, as well as Leak's extraordinary courage. Modestly, Leak waved off the accolades, insisting that everyone present deserved the medal for what *they* had done.

On the 16th of August the 9th moved on to Albert brickfields, where it rained heavily for days, turning their camp in to a field of slushy mud. During their so called respite, the heights of Pozieres had been taken and the line was slowly pushing forward towards Mouquet Farm, a ruined farm house on the crest of some high ground two thousand yards north north west of Pozieres and fifteen hundred yards west south west of Thiepval.

At the old British lines at Becourt Wood on the 19th of August, the battalion was issued with rations and water, then moved into the line at Mouquet Farm. The troops moved forward during daylight as there were no longer any identifiable landmarks, their route taking them through Pozieres village, where each man noted its thorough destruction. Not a single building remained, just piles of rubble reminding all that a town once stood here. The devastation was a harsh testament to the ferocity of the battles that had raged and were still raging in the area. As the soldiers advanced, they trod carefully over pock marked streets and crumbling foundations, the eerie silence amplifying the desolation around them. The once vibrant village had been reduced to a ghostly expanse, with shattered remnants of bricks and splintered wood scattered amidst the debris. The sight left a profound impact on the men, serving as a painful and sad reminder of the war's relentless destruction and the sacrifices made by those who had fought there.

'C' and 'D' Companies reached the front line around midnight, having marched along K Trench. As they advanced, the distant glow of explosions illuminated the night sky, revealing the terrifying reality ahead. Their destination was under an intense and seemingly endless artillery bombardment, and as they moved down from the ridge towards their trenches, the ground was shaking with each deafening blast; yet onwards they marched. As shells whistled overhead, the air was thick with smoke and the acrid smell of gunpowder, whilst the artillery fire found its mark more than once, with many a brave man being lost. But, despite the chaos and carnage, the soldiers pressed forward, ready to hold the line.

The 9th was allocated positions in front of Mouquet Farm, with the 12th Battalion to their right, in the centre of the 3rd Brigade line, and the 10th Battalion in situ on the brigade's right flank. The 11th Battalion, on this occasion, was the carrying party, a vital role in any battle, ensuring a constant flow of ammunition and supplies to the front line. Fabeck Graben was an enemy trench situated to the front of the brigade centre and right flank.

The 9th's new position in the line was not exactly ideal, consisting of three shallow trenches, only one of which, the right hand trench, being connected to the rest of the line. This unfortunate situation made the task of movement between trenches a dangerous and treacherous undertaking, not only for the front line battalions, but more so for the carrying parties.

The middle trench, however, had a thirty foot deep semi circular chalk quarry to its rear; a possible safe area or storage zone.

As 'B' Company arrived in the forward trench the officers and NCOs expected the usual briefing from the unit which they were relieving; but not today. The trench was a grim sight, with bodies scattered around and wounded soldiers in pain, lying there untreated. But what struck 'B' Company the most was the eerie silence. The survivors seemed lost, struggling to speak clearly or explain what had happened. The constant shelling from both sides had taken its toll. Most of the defenders had been killed or wounded, and those who were left were so mentally scarred by their ordeal that the relieving troops could get nothing intelligible from them. In fact the men could not get out of there any quicker.

"Hey, mate, what's the situation up here?" CSM McBride asked, addressing one of the defenders.

The soldier stared blankly for a moment before shaking his head.

"Can't...can't say...too much...too much noise...too much..."

Clancy exchanged a worried glance with Archie and Roo, who could see the fear etched in the soldier's eyes; the trauma of war leaving its mark.

"Alright, take it easy, son," Clancy said gently, placing a reassuring hand on the soldier's shoulder, "I'm sure we'll work it out."

'B' Company couldn't make much sense of what *any* of the men said, just that the soldiers were eager to leave as fast as they could.

"Come on, lad, you must know something," Archie urged

another man, his voice tinged with frustration, "we need to know what we're up against mate".

The soldier flinched at the sound of Archie's voice, his hands trembling as he struggled to find the right words.

"I...I can't...can't remember...everything's a blur..."

Archie sighed in frustration, feeling the weight of the situation bearing down on him. He glanced around at his mates, their expressions mirroring his own sense of unease.

"Any luck getting a briefing chaps?" Captain Ponsonby asked, joining his men as they surveyed the desolate scene.

The CSM shook his head, his expression ominous.

"Not much Freddy. Poor bastards. They're all in a right state and we can't seem to get a straight answer out of any of 'em".

Ponsonby sighed heavily, running a hand through his hair in frustration.

"Alright, let's concentrate on getting ourselves sorted then. We'll have to work things out as we go".

Feeling frustrated, 'B' Company focused on settling into the trench, fully aware that they had to be prepared for whatever came next.

Because of the heavy shelling, a decision was made to use as fewer troops as possible to hold the line.

"Good news boys. Us and 'A' Company are to be battalion reserve," announced Captain Ponsonby, "we're moving four hundred yards to the rear to a place called 'Fourth Avenue'. Let's get the men moving CSM".

"No worries skip," Clancy whispered as he signalled down the company line to move out.

'A' Company was to be located seven hundred yards to the rear, between a cemetery and a captured concrete strong post called Gibraltar. Battalion Headquarters was three hundred yards to the rear of the front line in 'Park Lane', whilst Brigade Headquarters was *in* Gibraltar.

During the night the three battle groups had set to work joining up and deepening the trenches. Success was minimal due to the hard chalky ground in parts, and loose earth in others falling back in to the diggings; made worse by the constant vibration caused by the shelling. Consequently, by dawn, the trenches were little more than knee deep.

There was much confusion on the front line. On the left flank of the 9th the area was open. Patrols were sent out to locate and link up with friendly forces, but none could be found.

"I hope Fritz doesn't see this bloody gap or he'll be through it, and we'll be for it," said Clancy.

There were a number of enemy OPs which proved too strong for patrols to destroy, and opposite was an enemy trench from which regular shooting and bombing came.

On Sunday the 20th of August shell fire was continuous on the front line. But at 1700 hours the barrage increased dramatically, with shells being concentrated between the forward and support trenches. This barrage was sporadic throughout the night, keeping all awake, and sending many to 'kingdom come'.

One of those casualties was John Leak, who had suffered a serious wound to the back during an artillery bombardment near the Gibraltar blockhouse. The strike came as a sudden, deafening roar, catching the men off guard as they huddled in their positions, shrapnel and debris flying in all directions, cries of pain and shock filling the air. Amidst the chaos, Leak's mates quickly realised he was down, calling frantically for stretcher bearers.

"Stretcher bearers! Over here, quick!" they shouted, while some tried to offer immediate aid, pressing cloths to his wound to stem the bleeding.

As Leak was being tended to, word of his injury quickly spread around the battalion, soldiers sheltering in their trenches, passing the news along the line in hushed tones.

"Hey boys have you heard, Leaky got wounded pretty bad by a shell?" announced Jacko.

Apart from the artillery, the silence from the men was deafening.

"Bloody hell!" exclaimed Archie, "I hope he is alright".

"Well, they're doing their best and have sent him to the rear," replied Jacko.

"At least he'll be out of it there, and a bit safer," sighed Roo.

"He'll be fine, the King wants to see him don't forget…you know, for his VC," added Taff.

Each man nodded in hope for their mate.

Although the heavy shelling died down at daybreak, the general bombardment was relentless. At one stage, on the 21st, the 9th was continually receiving rounds from a battery of the Royal Artillery, who were firing short.

The men of 'B' Company were bunched together in their reserve trenches; the rumble of artillery all around them. As Jacko peered over the parapet, suddenly a deafening explosion erupted nearby, sending dirt and debris flying, and Jacko diving back into the trench as he and his mates ducked for cover.

"What the bloody hell was that?!" exclaimed Jacko frantically.

As each soldier exchanged worried glances, another explosion shook the ground, the men suddenly realising the danger they were in.

"That's our own artillery, mate! They're firing short!" replied Archie, gritting his teeth.

Corporal Stowe shouted over the chaos.

"Get down, everyone! We need to contact those god damn gunners to adjust their aim!"

As Archie scrambled towards the field telephone Stowie grabbed a flare and rushed to the edge of the trench firing it into the air, the bright light cutting through the smoke and haze.

"CEASE FIRE! CEASE FIRE, DAMN IT!" he yelled as the flare slowly descended out of sight.

"They can't hear you mate. They're bloody miles away. Don't worry, Archie is on the blower to them now," said Clancy as he reassured the men.

Messages via the field telephone were constant to the Fire Control Centre, with calls of "CHECK YOUR FIRE!" Eventually they got the message.

There was no let up for anyone, with men constantly tending and evacuating the wounded, as well as digging out mates who had been buried.

The men were also suffering from a new 'wound' called shell shock. Strong men shaken to the core, being taken to a lean-to hut in the quarry for some respite; not that they were out of danger or earshot of the explosions of course, as artillery rounds landed indiscriminately around the Aussie lines.

The enemy OPs were very observant, watching out for troop movements, then laying special barrages on the routes they were taking; 'K' Trench being a prime example.

Again, at 1730 hours, another intense artillery bombardment fell on all of the Aussie lines, but the work of the front line troops, assisted by the reserve companies and pioneers, had paid off. After forty eight hours spent deepening their trenches, the light rate of casualties was a testament to their determination.

The 3rd Brigade attacked Mouquet Farm and Fabeck Graben in broad daylight. Artillery strikes had been rehearsed prior to the attack. Misleading preliminary bombardments had been made but not followed up by storming infantry as expected, thus confusing the enemy.

Originally the 9th were to be one of the attacking battalions but it was considered that an attack to its front was hopeless. 'A' Company, however, *would* be taking part.

Clancy was not a happy man at the news.

"Hopeless?!" he exclaimed, "So, what are *we* doing?"

"Providing covering fire old boy," replied Ponsonby.

"Covering fire?" growled Clancy, "it's bloody Lone Pine all over again!"

From 1330 to 1400 hours, the Royal Artillery relentlessly bombarded the enemy positions in preparation for the infantry assault. As the attack went in, it was accompanied by a meticulously planned creeping barrage. This artillery strategy involved a rolling curtain of shells, which first concentrated its fire for two minutes at a point half way to Fabeck Graben. After that, the barrage shifted and focused its destructive power directly on Fabeck Graben for three minutes before lifting to target positions further beyond. 'A' Company, alongside the 10th and 12th Battalions, initially reported the farm as captured but were forced to withdraw due to heavy shelling from both sides. The Germans, seizing the opportunity, wasted no time in swiftly re-occupying the farm.

The whole operation had been a difficult undertaking, what with many of the saps and communication trenches now caved in due to the heavy shelling, which continued throughout the following day. However, a thick morning fog *did* provide a welcome cloak under which supplies and men could be brought forward.

The men, who had been in the line now for three days, were so shaken by the shelling that they subsisted on water and cigarettes due to the impossible situation which did not allow for meal preparation...unless you wanted it to be your last. The relentless barrage of enemy artillery created an environment where even lighting a small fire to cook was tantamount to a death sentence. The constant explosions had the men on edge, their nerves frayed to breaking point, each man crouching in their trenches, clutching their rifles and praying for the bombardment to cease, their only comfort the shared misery and a cigarette passed between mates.

The artillery fire had been heavier than that at Pozieres the previous month, and all were now suffering from lack of sleep, fatigue, and hunger. The soldiers' eyes were sunken, and their faces gaunt, an indication of the ceaseless bombardment and the strain of constant vigilance. Finally, on the afternoon of the 22nd, the battalion was to be relieved, a moment they had been desperately awaiting. However, the relief battalions suffered heavy losses on the way in, caught in the same hellish artillery fire. The sight of fresh troops staggering into the lines, already depleted and bloodied, was a sobering reminder of the relentless nature of the war, yet despite their own exhaustion, the men of the 9th mustered what strength they had left to assist the incoming soldiers, knowing that their own brief respite depended on the successful relief of their positions.

For their three days at Mouquet Farm the 9th Battalion had lost twenty seven men killed, one hundred and twenty five wounded and a further twelve missing; the missing most likely either receiving a direct hit or being buried during an explosion. However, all in all, over nearly seven weeks of fierce battles at Pozières and Mouquet Farm, the Australian Imperial Force's three divisions endured a staggering twenty three thousand casualties, with six thousand eight hundred being killed or succumbing to wounds.

The battalion were now out of the line and heading to a reserve area. A couple of days march through Albert, Warloy, and on to Beauval did nothing for morale. After wearing their boots constantly for nearly a week, most were now plagued with sores and blisters on their feet.

As the Australian soldiers trudged wearily through the French countryside, the landscape around them was a mix of rolling fields, scattered villages, and dense patches of forest. The fields, once vibrant with life, now lay scarred by the ravages of war, with shell craters dotting the landscape like pockmarks on a weathered face. The villages they passed through bore the scars of war, their buildings damaged or destroyed, their streets littered with debris.

As they marched, the soldiers exchanged weary glances and occasional muttered words, their faces etched with fatigue and perseverance. Clancy, his weather-beaten face and a perpetually happy expression, marched at the head of 'B' Company with an unusually quiet resolve. Roo, like many of the men, although struggling, managed to keep up with the pace, his brow furrowed in pain from the blisters on his feet.

Roo's cousin Archie, tried to lighten the mood as they passed through a particularly desolate stretch of land.

"I hear there might be nurses to kiss our feet better when we get to wherever we're going".

"Yeah, well, they'll be needing a doctor themselves if they kiss your smelly feet then won't they?" Clancy quipped, earning a tired chuckle from his comrades.

Taff cast a concerned glance around the men as they limped along.

"We need to find a place to rest soon," he said, his Welsh accent thick with worry, "these blisters won't heal if we keep marching like this."

On the 25th the battalion marched in to Douellens, where they were relieved to see a train which would transport them on the next leg of their journey.

"Percy made a good choice eh Arch?" noted Clancy.

"Good choice?" Archie replied, scratching his head.

"You know, by joining the light horse," Clancy answered, "none of this flamin' foot sloggin' everywhere".

Stowie nodded in agreement.

"Thank goodness for the train ride. With our feet in this state we can't keep going like this forever," he said, his voice hoarse from days of shouting commands over the noise of the artillery.

The battalion was off to Flanders, the Dutch-speaking northern, region of Belgium, which since Roman times had seen nothing but war, primarily due to its flat geography and its crucial position along the entire Belgian coastline on the North Sea. At 0830 hours they detrained at a place called Proven, from where they formed up and marched to Poperinghe.

As they marched, the distant rumble of artillery fire reminded them of the battles yet to come. But for now, they pressed on, their spirits kept afloat by the mateship and banter of their fellow soldiers and the hope that their efforts would soon end this terrible war.

The battalion billet was a large warehouse on which was a sign saying Houblows, a French word for Hops, a major product in Flanders.

The 9th Battalion were now Divisional Reserve in the Ypres sector.

Ypres, an ancient town famed for its linen trade with England, had played a pivotal role in numerous treaties and battles throughout its history. In the current conflict, its strategic significance lay in blocking Germany's planned advance from

Belgium into France. Surrounded by the German army on three fronts, Ypres had endured relentless bombardment from the war's outset, prompting British, French, and allied forces to launch counteroffensives from the Ypres Salient.

By the end of 1914, the Allies had successfully reclaimed Ypres from German control during the First Battle of Ypres, but the Germans had introduced poison gas, specifically chlorine, on the 22nd of April 1915, targeting Canadian, British, and French troops. This marked the beginning of the Second Battle of Ypres, which lasted until the 25th of May 1915, resulting in the Germans securing higher ground to the town's east.

Clancy scratched his head.

"Bloody hell how do you say the name of *this* place…Yeeps!?"

"The Tommies call it Wipers," said Archie.

"Yeeps, Wipers, either way it's a strange name," replied Clancy.

"The correct pronunciation is ee-pruh apparently old boy," added Captain Ponsonby.

"Ee-pra…that's not too hard…thanks boss," said a grateful Clancy as he smiled with relief.

By the 12th of September the battalion had made several moves, including 'Connaught Lines' near Reninghelst, 'Devonshire Lines', a hutted camp east south east of Busseboom, to Brandhoek where they boarded a train to Ypres, and later marching the three miles to the front line in the Hill 60 sector west south west of Ypres. It hadn't all been marching though as the Battalion Fund treated the men to tickets to a Division concert party performance, at a cost of one hundred and twenty Francs.

"Hey, Roo, Arch, you coming to the show?" called out Clancy, as he stood with Taff and Stowie.

"Wouldn't miss it for quids," replied Roo.

The theatre was a large tent, and the stage was nothing more than a couple of wooden crates stacked on top of each other, draped with a tattered Union Jack. A motley crew who had once trod the boards of grand theatres, and others who had honed their craft in more modest venues gathered backstage, tuning instruments and whispering nervous encouragements to each other.

The theatre buzzed with anticipation as soldiers crowded around, and as the audience settled onto the muddy ground, a Major, himself a veteran of the theatre, took to the stage with a flourish, a battered ukulele in hand.

"Welcome gentlemen, to the greatest show on the Western Front; an evening of entertainment fit for kings!" he announced, his voice booming over the crowd.

The audience cheered and whistled as the first act graced the rickety stage, but they weren't to be disappointed, for the performances that followed were evidence to the talent within the ranks of the concert party. Professional actors, who had enlisted just like their audience, *and* fought between performances, brought to life characters from distant lands, whilst comedians had the audience in stitches with their witty banter. There was even a juggler who, with a grand gesture, produced three potatoes from his pocket and attempted to juggle them with all the grace of a drunken elephant, the audience erupting into laughter as the potatoes went flying in all directions, narrowly missing a few heads in the front row.

But it was the female impersonators who stole the show. Dressed in extravagant costumes and wielding quick tongues, they brought a touch of glamour to the depressing surroundings of war torn Flanders, their bawdy sense of humour a welcome diversion from the harsh realities of war, lifting the spirits of soldiers, weary from nearly two years of fighting.

As the final act took to the stage with a makeshift ventriloquist dummy fashioned out of a sock and a potato, he had the audience roaring with laughter as he engaged in a mock conversation with his "companion."

Thunderous applause followed as Clancy suddenly felt the desire to tread the boards himself.

As he clambered up on to the stage he held up his hands to quieten down the audience, who thought the sergeant major had a serious announcement to make.

"Do any of you blokes like poetry?" Clancy asked.

As one, the audience sighed with relief.

"Well, I've got one for yous," said Clancy as he began his recitation, "there was a young ANZAC in Wipers, who was hit in the arse by two snipers, the songs that he played, from the holes that they made, were better than any Jock pipers".

Hails of laughter filled the tent as Clancy waved and bowed to his audience, the men bursting in to an impromptu chorus of 'Kiss Me Goodnight Sergeant Major'.

At their new positions the battalion relieved a regiment of Canadian and Newfoundland soldiers who had fought magnificently in this sector since the campaign had begun. But this area had now quietened down. Both sides were exhausted. Although battle weary, they wished the Aussies well and moved out of the trenches in an orderly fashion, each man expertly concealing his own personal torments and feelings of relief.

After their ordeal on the Somme, the Aussies had been sent to the Ypres sector for a well earned rest, with the enemy on the opposite side of no man's land there for the same purpose; resulting in a reasonably quiet period. However, there may not have been much fighting to be had, but there was plenty of work for every man.

"This must be one of Clancy and Freddy's famous rest periods like we had on Gallipoli!" exclaimed Roo.

Clancy's ears pricked up at the mention of his name.

"What?" he asked.

"I was just saying about your 'let's get tired parties' at Gallipoli," replied Roo.

"Oh yeah…those were the days eh, swimming at the cove," said Clancy as he dreamed of sunnier climes.

Roo glanced over their new position.

"Well at least we don't have far if we fancy a dip. Look at the state of the place; water everywhere," he said.

The trenches were indeed in a poor state and, despite much work to improve them, heavy rain had caused the parapets to cave in, and as the 9th discovered, the only way to shore them up was sandbagging with over five thousand sandbags; which worked a treat.

However, this didn't help in the front line trenches where there was mud and water up to the knees, so, to combat this, every man was issued with thigh length rubber boots.

It was autumn now, but autumn in northern Europe was very different from Queensland where it signalled the end of the summer rains and more manageable temperatures, for here it was suddenly upon them, becoming bitter cold, as if summer had turned straight in to winter.

"Bloody hell! I thought Gallipoli was cold," exclaimed Clancy.

"Ah, but this isn't cold dear boy. The worst is yet to come," replied Captain Ponsonby.

"Thanks mate. You really know how to cheer a fella up," laughed Clancy as he rubbed his freezing hands together, then interlocked his fingers and began breathing warm air into his clenched fists.

The front line in the sector was lightly manned as a result of the high number of casualties in full trenches being caused by the heavy shelling. War and tactics it seemed were evolving for the better, with much common sense being used for a change. As a result, the front line trenches were occupied by two hundred men for every thousand yards. Here they manned strong points and patrolled the trenches between each one. Meanwhile, in the support trenches which ran almost parallel, three hundred yards to the rear, four hundred men per one thousand yards were constantly at a heightened state of readiness.

This particular area was like an ant colony, with a myriad of mine tunnels being excavated by both sides; the 'worker ants' being employed to fetch and carry timber and explosives.

A rest area it may have been, but patrols were still sent out each night.

On the 17th of September Captain Ponsonby held an 'O' Group. A fighting patrol of five scouts, two bombing teams and one Lewis Gun team were being sent out.

"Roo, I want you and your section to recce the enemy

trenches to the battalion front," said the captain, "it seems that they are unoccupied during daylight, but manned at night".

"And you want us to confirm this?" replied Roo.

"Yes. Yes I do. The particular trench we are interested in is this one," said Ponsonby as he pointed to a position marked on his map, "if you can get to it before the Germans occupy it for the night, then it's ours".

"And one step forward for us eh?" Roo noted.

"Exactly...so good luck my friend, and make sure you see the CSM for ammunition and bombs," relied Ponsonby, shaking Roo's hand.

Back in the reserve trench Roo briefed his patrol, each man indicating their understanding of the mission.

"There's one problem sarge," said Taff, "no Lewis Gun".

"Bloody hell, we'd better remedy that then," replied Roo.

"Already have," came a familiar voice from around one of the zig zag bends in the trench.

It was Clancy, Lewis Gun in hand and ammunition party in tow.

"Ripper!" said Taff, his arms held out for the machine gun.

Clancy gave him a surprised look.

"You can bugger off Taff, this is mine!" exclaimed the CSM, "I'm coming with yer".

"I don't think the OC will be too pleased with that," said Roo.

"Well, what he doesn't know won't hurt him," replied the CSM.

"If anything happens to you he won't be happy," said Taff.

"...and I *won't*?!" snapped Clancy, a cheeky smile etched on his face.

With the seasons changing, the days were becoming shorter, so the patrol didn't have to wait for the usual 2200 hours dusk.

Faces blackened, rattling and shining items removed or covered, Roo's patrol quietly made their way along the communication sap to the forward trench.

Archie was one of the sergeants detailed to the strong point that evening so the patrol had a pleasant surprise when they reported to him.

As he leaned against the trench wall, his gaze scanning the faces of the soldiers before him, he raised his eyebrow, a smirk playing on his lips, and addressed the group.

"Well, well, what do we have here? Planning a midnight jaunt, are we?"

Taff, ever quick with a retort, straightened up with a grin.

"Aye, Sarge, just thought we'd take a leisurely stroll through no man's land; thought the stars might be nice this time of night."

Archie chuckled quietly, shaking his head in mock disapproval.

"Ah, yes, nothing like a moonlit promenade among the craters and barbed wire. Mind you don't trip over any surprises left by old Fritz," said Archie.

"Promenade? Whatever that is...you're starting to sound more like Freddy every day mate," replied Clance.

"Clance? Sorry mate I didn't see you there".

Clancy eyed the Lewis Gun which he was carrying.

"Yeah, we've packed a picnic just in case. We thought we'd share it with our friends across the wire."

"Well, isn't that thoughtful of you? Perhaps you'll even trade recipes while you're at it," Archie joked.

Private "Ten Bob" Kropp, his nerves betraying him with a shaky smile, joined in the banter.

"Maybe we'll bring back some souvenirs for you, Sarge. A nice helmet or a bit of shrapnel, perhaps?"

Archie laughed quietly whilst clapping a hand on Kropp's shoulder, then looking over to Clancy.

"Have you been leading young Kroppy here astray Clance?" Archie replied, "now that's the spirit, Kroppy, but just be sure to bring yourselves back in one piece, and don't get lost…righto boys what's your password for tonight?"

"Wombat," replied Roo.

"Wombat? That's a strange one mate," said Archie.

"Yeah…I thought that it's not a word the Germans would know or be able to pronounce," replied Roo.

"Too right boyo, they'd probably say vombat, or the like," laughed Taff.

"Righto, I'll let the blokes know," replied Archie, as he eyed each man, whilst giving a nod to Clancy and Roo, "I'll see you when I see you".

Darkness was almost upon them as the patrol slipped stealthily over the parapet. Once in no man's land the bombing teams moved on to the flanks of their diamond formation, and Clancy, with his machine gun, placed himself in the centre, ensuring he could easily step to the left or right should his gun be required. Roo felt uneasy as the group edged forward, holding up his left hand, giving the signal to halt. Pausing for just a moment he strained his eyes, trying to see in the darkness. Something wasn't right and each man could feel it too. Signalling for his men to lie prone, the patrol began to crawl across the shell scarred terrain towards the enemy trench, edging closer and closer. Then, from out of the darkness came several thudding sounds, like huge hailstones crashing to the ground. A storm-like downpour of stick grenades had rained down on all sides of the group, their explosions sending shrapnel flying in all directions. Roo's signal to crawl had saved their lives as the grenade fragments flew over the heads of their intended victims. Each man now froze as more bombs landed near them. Then, something they did not want...flares! The immediate area was now lit up like the main street in town. Still frozen in position the patrol could not be seen, but the Aussies did see about fifty Germans advancing towards them in the illuminated night.

"Stupid bastards," Roo whispered to himself, as he spoke calmly and quietly to the patrol, "everyone hold your fire and prepare to withdraw, "gun group, twenty yards, enemy platoon at one o'clock, bursts...FIRE!"

"I thought he'd never ask," said Clancy to Kropp, who was acting as his number two, "get ready with those mags because I'm ripping into them".

Flicking out his bipod and quickly training his gun on the right of the enemy line, Clancy squeezed the trigger and let fly from right to left with his full magazine of forty seven rounds. As he drilled into them, the Germans fell like dominoes, some screaming, others falling silently, killed instantly by the hail of lead from Clancy's muzzle.

"RELOAD!" Clancy shouted to Private Kropp as the soldier expertly released the empty magazine and clipped on a full one.

"Ready when you are!" Clancy shouted to Roo.

"This time bursts mate, bursts!" shouted Roo.

As Clancy opened fire again, this time with bursts of two or three rounds at a time, Roo shouted to his men.

"GET BACK FOR YOUR LIVES! GO! GO!!"

Immediately each man rose to their feet, turned, and sprinted as fast as their legs could carry them, to the safety of the Aussie forward trench, calling out "WOMBAT!" as they ran. Still firing from the hip, Clancy, with his face and weapon towards the enemy, moved back in a sort of trot, guided by his number two, who grasped his belt from the rear and dragged him steadily back to the Aussie lines. As they reached the safety of their trench, each man jumped in or lowered himself down, without a single casualty or shot being let off by the Germans. Clancy, however, was a different story as he defiantly emptied his magazine in one continuous burst, spraying left and right towards the enemy trench, then, simply dropping nonchalantly back in to the battalion trench.

Private Kropp was now coming in to his own as a soldier, and Clancy could see it.

"Good on yer Ten Bob, that was a good night's work," he said as he patted Kropp on the shoulder.

8

Pack up your troubles

On the 30th of September the 1st Light Horse Brigade moved on to Kantara for a six week spell where again it was a time of revision, fitness and rest. During this period all of the officers were sent to Cavalry School, whilst the troops were permitted the odd day off in Alexandria and Port Said; in batches of twenty.

"There's justice eh?" said Chugger.

"What do you mean?" asked Trooper 'Johnno' Whitby, one of the latest re-enforcements from Australia.

"Well Johnno me old mate, at Gallipoli, every time we were taken out of the line we were used for manual labour," Chugger replied, "you know, digging saps and roads; all sorts".

"So, what do you mean by justice?" asked Johnno.

"He means that the officers *never* do the hard labour, but now *they're* working and *we're* not," interrupted Percy.

"Oh right. I like that sort of justice," replied Johnno.

"Don't we all mate?" added Davo.

Having experienced the delights of Alexandria already, the boys, along with their new mate Trooper Whitby, set their sights on Port Said, which lay on the coast of the Mediterranean Sea, at the mouth of the Suez Canal.

Transport, however, was scarce, but Percy had managed to find a local with a truck, which had seen better days, to act as a taxi…for a fee of course. After enduring a bone jarring journey on the rickety truck, that rattled and groaned its way across the dusty desert terrain, the Australian soldiers finally arrived in Port Said after a gruelling forty eight mile trek from the southern outpost of Kantara. Dust coated and weary, they clambered down from the back of the vehicle, stretching their cramped limbs and squinting against the glare of the sun.

"We'll see you here in five hours Mohammed," said Percy as he gave the driver a crisp one pound note, "and there'll be more money when we see you".

One pound was a lot of money, and Mohammed was very grateful.

"Shukran jazeelan…thank you my friend…five hours," replied Mohammed, holding up five fingers, "I see you then. Ma'a assalama, Assalamu alaikum".

"What did he say mate?" asked Chugger.

"I'm pretty sure it was something like good bye and peace be upon you," replied Percy.

"Really? That's bloody kind," said Chugger as he grasped Mohammed's hand and shook it vigorously, "and the same to you mate. Good on yer".

Port Said was founded in the 1800s during the construction of the canal, the buildings with their grand balconies on all floors, giving the city a distinctive look, a mixture of Arab and European influences. Much like Cairo, Port Said greeted them with an explosion of sights and sounds, a striking contrast to the desolate expanses over which they had travelled to reach its bustling harbour. The waterfront teemed with activity as cargo ships loomed large against the deep blue horizon, their masts swaying gently in the sea breeze. Seagulls wheeled overhead, their cries mingling with the shouts of dockworkers as they unloaded crates and barrels from the vessels.

Having escaped the confines of their cramped vehicle, the soldiers set off to explore the vibrant streets of the port city. Along the busy thoroughfares, they encountered a myriad of sights and smells that spoke of the city's cosmopolitan charm. Exotic spices filled the air, mingling with the tang of saltwater and the pungent scent of fish drying in the sun.

As they made their way through the bustling marketplace, the soldiers found themselves accosted by persistent street peddlers, their wares displayed in colourful arrays that beckoned tantalizingly to passersby. The men, however, were not in the mood to be badgered today, so, with a mixture of amusement and irritation, the Australians brushed off the vendors with curt commands to "bugger off," their patience worn thin by the relentless haggling and cajoling.

Despite their weariness, the soldiers found solace in the sight of the shimmering Mediterranean Sea, its sapphire waters stretching out to the horizon, reminding them of home, and peaceful times that lay behind them.

"That's more like it boys," said Davo as he surveyed the beautiful coastline.

Feeling relieved, they made their way to the shoreline, kicked off their heavy boots, rolled up their trousers and waded into the cool embrace of the sea. As they paddled, splashed and frolicked in the gentle waves, the men exchanged jokes and laughter, the cares of the world almost melting away, as they momentarily let thoughts of war drift out of sight and mind.

Relaxing on the sandy beach the boys thought of Australia.

"We haven't been home for two years now," said Percy.

"Yeah...so much for it will all be over by Christmas eh?" remarked Chugger.

"Ah, but they didn't say *which* Christmas though did they?" replied Davo.

"I wonder how much longer it will last though?" asked Percy.

"Who knows mate?" replied Boggy, "and as me old mum used to say, it's not worth dwelling on".

"No. You're right mate," said Percy, looking over to Trooper Whitby, "hey Johnno, where are you from?"

"Me? I'm from Wondai," replied Johnno, "it's a small settlement out near Murgon and Kingaroy".

"Yeah? What do you do out there?" asked Davo.

"I'm just a stockman mate," replied Johnno.

"Hey mate, no one's *just* a stockman. It's us stockman who *make* the light horse what it is," replied Percy.

"Here, here!" added Boggy.

"Is anyone hungry?" asked Chugger.

"Bloody hell mate have you got the tape worm or something?!" exclaimed Davo.

"A man's got to eat mate," replied Chugger as he spied a street seller about fifty yards away, "come on boys, let's see what they've got".

The others weren't too sure, having heard stories of rampant diarrhoea following the consumption of Arab street food.

"Come on fellas," said Chugger as he ushered his mates towards the stall, "it'll be fine, and besides I would much rather eat something that is freshly prepared in front of me".

"I suppose you're right," replied Percy as he eyed a couple of meals that he recognised, "yeah I reckon I'll give it a go".

Johnno, who had yet to sample the culinary delights of Egypt, was curious as he looked over the stall.

"Er...excuse me mate," he said to the vendor, "can you tell me what these dishes are please?"

"Certainly syid," replied the kindly vendor, "this is khoshary and this is ta'ameya. Khoshary is pasta and pulses with a tomato sauce, and ta'ameya is a falafel made with fava beans, and you put it all inside this bread".

Johnno inhaled the spicy aromas, the scent of which made his mouth water.

"If it tastes as good as it smells then I will be happy. I'll have one of each please," said Johnno, holding out a handful of coins, which the vendor politely waved away.

"No, no. I cannot accept your money. You are Australia...yes? You have come from far away to help us. That is payment enough. I would be offended to take your money".

"What's your name mate?" enquired Percy.

"Malik," replied the man.

Percy offered his hand in friendship, which Malik gladly accepted.

"Listen Malik, where we come from we pay our dues. We can't accept this," said Percy, to nods of agreement from the others.

Malik then beckoned Percy closer and whispered in his ear.

"Do not worry syid," he said as he pointed to a large group of British soldiers who were heading towards his stall, "see those Tommies? I charge them double to make up my losses".

Percy chuckled to himself as Malik quickly served up the food to the five Aussies, thanked them for their business and waved them on their way.

After a relaxing afternoon it was soon time to meet up with Mohammed for the bumpy ride back to camp.

On the Western Front, the German army were equipped with the Minenwerfer trench mortar, which had been nick named the "Minnie" by the allied troops due to the moaning noise it made as it travelled through the air. It fired a two foot by nine inches sausage shaped round, also with a nick name, the "rum jar". Meanwhile, the Empire troops had the Stokes Mortars and Rifle Grenades, which were more than enough of a response to the clumsy, yet deadly, enemy offering; clumsy in the fact that the missile was large and slow and the men could literally see it coming, thus giving them a fighting chance of removing themselves from its impact area.

As well as the various weapons to be aware of, it was also the expertise behind some of those weapons which was of concern. As on the peninsula, snipers were an ever present danger, with trench periscopes being "killed" no sooner had they been raised above the parapet.

"There's no such thing as peering over the top here boys; you wouldn't last a minute," remarked Taff to his section.

When not fighting, watching or sleeping, the men of the battalion were constantly on the go, digging or repairing trenches, fetching and carrying. As Roo chopped in to the earth with his entrenching tool yet another rotting corpse was exposed. To the uninitiated civilian this would have been a traumatic experience, but to the war hardened soldiers, it was a part of daily life.

"Aye, aye, looks like another Tommy chum...poor beggar," said Roo very calmly as he pointed to the unfortunate individual.

"Gis a gander," said an eager Ten Bob who, although in the last few months had seen death at first hand, was curious at how a decaying body might look.

"Strewth! That's enough to put you off yer bully beef," he observed, sniffing the air, "in fact, he *smells* a bit like bully...go on have a wiff".

Stowie wasn't impressed, curling his top lip and raising an eye brow.

"You really are a strange fella Kroppy," announced Stowie, "where I'm from they'd call you el loco".

"Strange or not, show some respect. This is someone's son,

brother or husband. His family have probably been told that he is missing, so at least now they can have *some* peace," said Roo.

As the men dragged the body from its 'grave', they noticed that he had been chewed quite badly by the large and hairy rats which occupied the battlefield.

"The rats in yere are greedy buggers," said Taff, in his broad Welsh accent, "I caught one chewing on my puttees while I was trying to sleep. Woke me up he did".

Following five days at Halifax camp, two miles east of Busseboom, then another six days at Chateau Belge south east of Ypres, the 9th relieved the 10th Battalion in the line. As this was a suspected enemy mine centre, the trenches were lightly manned. In places the enemy trenches were only twenty five yards away, but it wasn't the Germans who were the problem, it was the severely dilapidated trenches and the rain and mud. After seven days the 9th were relieved by the 7th, and spent the next four days at Dominion Camp, a mile north of Ouderdom, from here they had a three day march to Bayenghem-Les-Eperleques, and it was here that the troops were given the opportunity to vote in the conscription referendum.

"These flamin' politicians can't make a decision. You wait til we get home…I won't be voting for 'em!" growled Clancy.

"I agree mate. We need help and it's about time every able bodied bloke put their hands up to fight," said Archie.

"But do you think they'd fight as hard if they were forced to do it?" added Roo.

"They'd bloody have to mate...do or die...isn't that what the poem says?" replied Clancy.

But the vote was to be a disappointment for the troops who voted 72399 for, and 58984 against, because, despite *their* overwhelming majority, it was the voters back home who had the final say.

"Bloody do gooders!"

The weather was getting colder, with heavy morning frosts. The 20th of October saw the battalion move out to the Somme, their impending return bringing thoughts and visions to each soldier of the constant artillery bombardments which they had endured at Pozieres.

Arriving at Fricourt four days later, after travelling on foot, by train *and* motor bus, it was cold, raining and muddy. Each man could not help recall that when they were last here, Fricourt was more or less on the front line, but now it was five miles to the rear.

"Five miles!" exclaimed Clancy, "some bloody good work has been done here".

Thankfully, as part of the 1st Division, the battalion remained in reserve for a week.

In the dim light of the reserve trench, the Australian soldiers bunched together, their faces illuminated by the occasional flickering of flares arcing across the night sky, as they tended to their boots. Some sat with their legs crossed, diligently scrubbing away the mud and grime, while others carefully applied dubbin, a waxy substance, which helped to waterproof the leather, their movements methodical and precise. The air was thick with the scent of earth and dampness, mingling with the faint aroma of tobacco from the odd cigarette here and there. The only sound was the quiet rustling of letters being opened, and snippets of conversation drifting through the trench like whispers on the wind.

"Oy, Clance, reckon this dubbin will hold up in the next downpour?" said Roo.

Clancy grinned and nodded.

"Aye, mate, worked a charm last time. Keeps the water out better than a dam wall".

Nearby, Taff chuckled, his voice tinged with a hint of homesickness.

"I can't wait to see what me mam has written this time; probably complaining about the weather being too hot back home again."

His mates laughed; the sound carrying a warmth that momentarily dispelled the chill of the trench.

"So did you come to Australia with your parents?" asked Roo.

"Yes boyo, ten years ago, when I was twelve. The prospects seemed better for us than back home," replied Taff, "my mam and da opened a general store and tea rooms in town and they are doing well. Better than working down the mines for a pittance that's for sure".

Further down the line, 'Ten Bob' Kropp, the youngest of the lot sat apart from the group, his brow furrowed in concentration as he struggled with a stubborn envelope.

"Blasted thing won't open," he muttered under his breath, earning sympathetic chuckles from his mates.

Roo sat down next to Ten Bob and tapped him on the shoulder.

"Here, let me have a go at it mate. Reckon I've got a knack for wrestling with annoying envelopes".

Clancy looked up and smiled mischievously at Roo, who noticed that Clancy was about to grace them with a witty comment.

"Don't even think about it Clance," said Roo as he eyed his mate up and down.

Clancy held his open hands out and said nothing.

As Roo deftly opened the envelope with a flourish, Ten Bob's face lit up with gratitude, and he eagerly unfolded the letter, devouring the words penned by his loved ones from across the sea, but a sombre expression clouded his features as he folded the paper, with a sigh, before tucking it into his tunic pocket.

"Everything alright mate?" asked Clancy, concern etched in his voice.

Ten Bob looked up and offered a tight-lipped smile.

"Yeah, just missin' home, ya know? Can't wait to be back on Aussie soil".

"Me neither," replied Clancy.

There was a chorus of agreement from the others, each sharing their own dreams of returning to the sunburnt country that they held so dear. As the night wore on, the trench gradually fell silent as the soldiers continued their tasks, finding comfort in the familiar routines of army life.

All areas of the Somme were now a muddy quagmire with the

mucky dark brown, or grey, sludge, being several inches deep. It wasn't unusual for a man to put his foot in the mud and leave his boot, sock, and occasionally his trousers behind, as the mud sucked at everything that ventured into it.

Again trench foot became a problem due to feet being constantly wet and cold. Whale oil was found to be a good preventative measure, being simply rubbed on the feet. Each man was also issued with three pairs of socks, thus ensuring a clean pair was available each day.

"Great, we just need somewhere clean to wash them," moaned Taff.

"I agree mate. I don't think that they think of those sorts of things, but hey, at least we have more socks eh?" added Stowie.

On the 30th of October the battalion was on the move again, but so, it appeared, was everyone else, as the four mile march to Bernafay Wood took almost six hours due to the motor vehicle congestion on the road, and the two foot deep mud on the verges. The battalion had to weave in and out of the traffic on the road in order to make any headway, and to further enflame the situation their destination was found to be a sea of slushy mud.

It rained constantly throughout the night, but as dawn broke, the relentless rain began to taper off, leaving a damp mist hanging over the trenches. The skies soon brightened to reveal over twenty observation balloons, tethered like sentinels, floating gracefully, rising high above the desolate landscape, and seemingly defying gravity. The sky was also alive with aircraft, a new sight for many, darting and circling, their engines roaring defiantly against the silence of the morning.

But, despite the modern ingenuity that was before them, there was a shortage of water; even though the shell craters all around them were overflowing with the stuff. No one dared to drink from the muddy shell holes as they were uncertain of what lay at the bottom...perhaps a rotting corpse.

The 1st of November brought yet another move, this time to Pommieres Camp, a few miles back; another sea of mud! But, despite their somewhat soggy surroundings there were *some* positives during their week long stay, the obvious being a break from battle, but the best came in the form of a small but significant comfort - the issue to each man of sheepskin vests and gloves. As each soldier received their bundle, there were murmurs of gratitude and relief, for these simple provisions offered a respite from the biting chill that permeated the camp. But perhaps the most welcome news of all was the announcement of a daily rum ration, with cheers erupting throughout the camp, a brief moment of celebration, and a reminder that even in the bleakest of times, there were small joys to be found.

On the 4th of November as the aroma of brewing tea mingled with the crisp morning air, the arrival of a Tank brought a rare moment of excitement. The Tank was a British invention, so named for its codename during its development, in an attempt to convince the enemy that they were devising some sort of new water tank. The Mark I, introduced to the battlefield only two months prior was the world's first tank, designed to traverse difficult terrain, crush barbed wire, and cross trenches while being resistant to machine gun and small arms fire. Its unusual rhomboidal shape allowed it to cross wide trenches, and decimate the enemy with its side mounted armaments of six pounder cannons and machine guns. This was a first sighting of the beast for the 9th Battalion and, despite the sodden mire which engulfed the camp, the soldiers gathered eagerly as the colossal machine lumbered through their midst. Heads turned, and murmurs of curiosity rippled through the camp as the strange silhouette loomed along the muddy track, easily gliding through the eighteen inches of mud. It was a marvel unlike anything they had ever encountered - a massive metal beast, its form both alien and awe-inspiring as it trundled towards them with a ponderous grace. Excitement crackled in the air as the soldiers crowded together to witness the spectacle unfolding before them. Wide-eyed and eager, they watched as the tank rolled closer, its tracks churning up waves of mud in its wake. There was no fear among them, only a sense of wonder at this extraordinary machine, and as the Tank rumbled past, the soldiers pressed forward for a better view, their faces alight with fascination as they marvelled at its sheer size and power, exchanging animated chatter and speculation about its capabilities. For these Aussie diggers the sight of the Tank represented a glimpse into a future where warfare was defined by innovation and technology.

"That was amazing!" exclaimed Stowie, "it was like a suit of armour on wheels".

"Yeah, well hopefully they'll be able to work out a good way to make use of them," Clancy murmured, not feeling all that optimistic about the new machine, "and they need to do something about the noise that it makes too, bloody squealing along like a pig with a hot poker up its backside!"

By the 9th of November, the battalion had returned to the front line, stationed at Flers, nestled in the Somme valley of France, amidst a region stretching from the Bocage to the Écouves forest. This area enjoyed a temperate climate shaped by its closeness to the English Channel and boasted a rich history dating back to the twelfth century. The de Flers family had wielded authority over the land since the tenth century, with Flers Castle, erected over seven hundred years ago, assuming significance during the French Revolution as a bastion for counter-revolutionary factions.

Today was a different story and a castle was no longer protection from ones enemies. Indeed the front line at Flers was a precarious one for it was not continuous, with a two hundred yard gap on the right flank between the 9th and 10th Battalions, and a hundred yards gap on the left. The fire trench was in a pitiful state as well, with twelve inches of thick and sticky mud at the bottom, with some spots being over two feet deep. Even Clancy managed to come a cropper as he trudged along the trench, as his boots sank deep into the thick, sticky mud that seemed determined to slow his progress. But, with a resigned sigh, he pushed onward, determined to force his way forward despite the treacherous conditions. As he struggled through the muck, Clancy felt his foot suddenly become lodged in the mud, causing him to stumble forward with a yelp of surprise. For a moment, he teetered on the edge of losing his balance, his heart racing as he fought to regain his footing. But instead of succumbing to panic, he let out a hearty laugh, the sound echoing through the desolate trench.

"There must be blokes buried in here," he called out to his

mates, flashing them a grin as he tried to extricate himself from the mud's clutches, "I'm sure one of the bastards is trying to nick my boots".

His mates, far from alarmed, erupted into laughter, their voices carrying through the gloom as they joined in the jest.

"Think you'll need a hand there, Clancy?" Roo called out, his tone laced with amusement.

"Nah, I reckon I'm right mate," Clancy replied with a wink, redoubling his efforts to free his foot from the mud.

Finally, with a squelching sound, he managed to wrench it free, stumbling forward a few paces before regaining his balance. As he rejoined his mates, they slapped him on the back, their laughter mingling with the distant artillery.

The rain pelted down thick and fast like a tropical Queensland downpour, but in the muddy fire trench there was no shelter, so the men had to stand, unless they were fortunate enough to find a protruding ammo box or other item to sit on. Once the rain subsided parties were organised to scoop out and toss the mud over the top, thus deepening the trenches whilst simultaneously raising the height of the parapet. Within a few days the front line trench was clear of mud...for now, as the rain, and mud, soon returned. The freezing weather didn't help either and soon there was sickness; mostly trench foot, which was combated through regular foot inspections and the use of whale oil. Nonetheless, the battalion numbers were dwindling due to the more severe cases having to be evacuated to the rear.

Shelling over the past few days had been light, but reasonably accurate. Luckily though there were few casualties in the battalion, however there *were* two encounters with the enemy when a

German aircraft was brought down in front of the 9th's lines and next when two German soldiers wandered into a freshly dug sap and gave themselves up.

The OC was not happy and as the German artillery fire momentarily subsided, Captain Ponsonby quickly peered over the parapet, binoculars in hand, scanning the horizon on the enemy side.

Clancy was concerned for his mate when he saw the dangerous position he was putting himself in.

"Careful skipper, there's still snipers out there. What yer doin' anyway?" he asked.

"Got yer you swine," whispered Ponsonby as he slid back down in the trench, then turned to the CSM, "I'm looking to see if there are any obvious high points for artillery observers".

"Did you find any?" asked Clancy, "The ground isn't that *high* round here".

"Yes, I think I did," replied Captain Ponsonby, offering Clancy his binoculars, "here take a look, just out on the horizon; you can just about make it out in the haze".

As Clancy scanned the distant ground a broad grin stretched across his face, for he had seen what his OC had spotted, a tower of some sort which was most likely being used by the Germans for artillery spotting.

"You clever bastard Fritz," said Clancy as he handed back the binoculars, "no wonder their shooting is so good".

"Yes, and time to do something about it," replied Ponsonby as he picked up the field telephone.

"What are you doing, ringing to ask the Germans politely to stop?" joked Clancy.

"Better than that, I'm calling for a Forward Observation Officer to come up here and take a look, then perhaps bring down some indirect fire on the blighters," Ponsonby replied.

Ponsonby's telephone call worked a treat, the FOO being very impressed with his sighting and being eager to remove the offending tower.

"So, sir, how are you going to do it? It will take a lot of guns to knock that thing down," enquired Clancy.

"It's all elementary sergeant major, I shall call in the big guns of the Royal Navy who are sitting twiddling their thumbs off the coast," replied the artillery Captain.

Clancy nodded in approval as the Captain relayed the grid reference of the tower to the Fire Control Centre, and within minutes there was a screaming and whooshing overhead as a single round scored a direct hit, reducing the tower to a pile of rubble.

Many of the ANZAC soldiers stood in awe as the distant structure crumbled to the ground before their eyes.

"That was bloody amazing sir. Can I shake your hand?" said a stunned Clancy.

"It's all part of the service," replied the cheery Captain as he shook hands with Clancy, Ponsonby and all within reach, "I must come here more often...toodle pip".

The light, and now less accurate, shelling allowed the men to carry out improvements on their trenches, adding overhead shelter and a new, closer line dug for the support company. This new corridor also allowed for the movement of certain luxuries, like hot food, with stew and tea being brought up the line by the cooks and Q Staff. Huge metal flask like containers holding enough for forty men, were strapped to the soldiers' backs. It was a struggle through the mud with containers, rifle and ammunition, but they made it.

"Look lads, here comes something good," Private Kropp exclaimed, wiping the sweat from his brow as he watched the cooks approach.

"Aye, thank the heavens for the cooks," replied Corporal Stowe, his stomach growling in anticipation, "I was starting to forget what hot food tasted like."

Grateful murmurs rippled through the ranks as the soldiers caught sight of the steaming flasks. Despite the slippery and muddy conditions and the weight of their burdens, the cooks and Q Staff battled on, determined to bring a moment of comfort to their mates on the front line.

"Stew and tea, just what the doctor ordered," remarked Archie, clapping a hand on Jacko's shoulder, "nothing like a hot meal to lift the spirits, as mum would say, eh?"

With muffled cheers of appreciation, the soldiers eagerly gathered around as the flasks were opened, releasing the tantalizing aroma of hearty stew and freshly brewed tea, and, for a brief moment, there was a semblance of normality as the soldiers savoured this small reprieve from the hardships of the trenches.

"God bless the cooks, I say," muttered Taff between mouthfuls of stew, "I don't know how you blokes manage to keep us fed in this mess".

"It aint always easy but we try our best," replied one of the cooks.

As the cooks moved along the trenches they were met with much, well deserved, gratitude, for despite their usual non combatant status they were performing a necessary task to keep the infantrymen going; whilst still suffering the same dangers and poor living conditions. And for that, the front line soldiers were truly grateful.

As for Archie, Roo and the boys, they sat bunched together to keep warm, whilst sharing stories and laughter over their makeshift meal, a sense of mateship filling the air.

9

We'll drink a cup of kindness yet

On the 13th of November 1916, the final phase of the Somme offensive began with the objective of seizing the Le Transloy Ridge. Field Marshal Douglas Haig's troops had previously attempted to secure this crucial position, but were impeded by heavy rain, which transformed the battlefield into a quagmire. The movement of artillery and infantry through the mud became exceptionally difficult. Moreover, adverse weather conditions hampered reconnaissance flights by the Royal Flying Corps due to poor visibility caused by rain and low hanging clouds. In contrast to the French, who were winding down operations for the winter, Haig's forces had not yet established secure positions, and given the vulnerable situation of British forces in flooded low ground, exposed to German observation, a renewed effort to capture the Le Transloy Ridge became imperative.

The 9th Battalion did not participate in this major offensive. However, there was an artillery feint on their front intended to divert attention away from the assault and capture, on their left flank, of St Pierre Divion and Beaumont Hamel by the 5th Army.

Following a fierce battle, Beaucourt was seized on the 14th of November. Despite initial concerns from Haig, General Gough secured approval for a final advance on the 18th of November, aiming to secure ground beyond Beaucourt for establishing advantageous winter positions. The infantry endured severe conditions exacerbated by snow and sleet, with much of the battlefield now resembling a featureless bog covered in ice. Visibility was severely limited as troops from five divisions advanced.

Although Australian, British, and Canadian forces made headway south of the Ancre to near Grandcourt, the tactical situation remained largely stagnant, hardly justifying the staggering twenty two thousand casualties incurred. Haig reluctantly halted the offensive, acknowledging that the weather and deteriorating ground conditions presented as significant obstacles as the German Army. Allied commanders ultimately realised that the Somme offensive no longer offered a realistic chance of achieving a decisive victory.

The 9th Battalion moved out of the line on the evening of the 13th of November, via the newly dug communication trench, to Bernafay Wood, then, on to Fricourt to a nissen hutted camp. Here they gratefully received a batch of reinforcements. After another four days the battalion marched to Buire, and the next day, were bussed to Cardonette near Amiens for a bit of sightseeing.

As the Australians strolled through the streets of Amiens, their conversations resonated with awe and curiosity about the town's many wonders.

"This reminds me a bit of our pony ride to Myrina when we were on Lemnos," said Clancy.

"Oh yeah, I'd forgotten about that. It seems like a lifetime ago now," replied Roo.

"Yeah it was a good day. Shame about our rocks though; I'm still annoyed about that," added Archie.

"Rocks? Why are you annoyed?" asked Clancy, scratching his head.

"You know the ones we kept as souvenirs. Mine was in my pack and went on walkabout on the first day at Gallipoli," replied Archie.

"I've still got mine…look," said Clancy as he reached in to his tunic pocket, "here you go 'Mates Together, Lemnos 1915'. I've kept it on me ever since".

"Me too. Mine's in one of my webbing pouches," said Roo.

Archie held out his hand to Clancy.

"Gis a squiz then…come on toss it over," he said.

As Archie caught the rock and held it in his hand, he paused for a second and recalled happier times before any of them had been baptised into the violence of warfare. A shiver radiated down his spine and he quickly passed the rock back to Clancy.

"Brrrrr! That was a strange and cold feeling. I'm glad you've both kept them though. Something to remind us of all of this eh?" said Archie.

The three men stood for a moment, the mood sombre, the thoughtful atmosphere being broken by the arrival of Taff and Stowie. Roo chuckled at Stowie's excitement.

"Have you fellas seen the cathedral yet?" Stowie called out as he and Taff joined the three mates, "it's absolutely amazing, towering above everything else".

"I didn't realise you were interested in architecture mate," said Roo.

"I've never been to Europe before and they aint got nothin' like this in Texas that's for sure," Stowie replied, "and after the last few months this place is like stepping into another world, so peaceful and green".

"Hey, I bet you didn't know that Jules Verne lived here?" said an excited Archie.

The rest of the mates shrugged their shoulders and looked baffled.

"He's a famous author…it's incredible to think that he walked these very streets," Archie added.

"What did he write about?" asked Taff.

"Well he was way ahead of his time and wrote about submarines, and rockets that travelled to the moon," replied Archie.

Clancy scoffed.

"Rockets to the moon…that'll never happen".

As they continued their walk, they marvelled at the vibrant quarters of Saint-Leu and Saint-Maurice, and sampled local delicacies such as macarons d'Amiens, and tuiles amienoises, which were chocolate and orange biscuits.

"These are bloody marvellous," announced Clancy as he stuffed his fifth macaron in to his mouth.

"Who's the fat guts now then?" joked Stowie as he eyed Clancy's belly.

It was not only the sweet treats which they enjoyed, as they swooned over the mouth watering duck paté in pastry and the la ficelle Picarde; an oven-baked crêpe with cheese.

This was *real* comfort food, and a far cry from army rations. But all good things must come to an end, and for these Aussie soldiers, Amiens was more than just a town on their journey, it was a touch of wonder, and a brief escape from the horrors of war.

The next eleven days were spent training and getting the new men ready for what lay ahead; followed by a four day march to Bazentin-Le-Grande where, for eight days, the battalion lived in tented accommodation and acted as fatigue parties. But, as winter descended upon the French and Belgian battlefields, the landscape transformed into a surreal, white expanse. Snow, a sight foreign to the Australian soldiers, fell softly, blanketing the trenches and no man's land alike. For many of these men, hailing from the sun drenched landscapes of Australia, this was their first encounter with snow, but the veterans who had faced the freezing temperatures and snowfall whilst clinging to the steep slopes of Gallipoli, had never witnessed anything like *this* enchanting snowfall, and even *they* stared in awe at the transformed world around them.

As Ten Bob stood at the side of his tent, his breath visible in the frigid air, a wide grin spread across his face.

"Crikey, would you look at that," he exclaimed.

Around him, his 'fair dinkum' mates murmured in amazement, their eyes reflecting a mix of wonder and curiosity. Conversations hummed through the camp, filled with exclamations of surprise and the inevitable comparisons to the harsh, sun baked deserts and lush, green coastlines of their homeland.

Laughter, however, soon broke out as the men, momentarily shedding their roles as soldiers, began to play. Snowball fights erupted spontaneously and Ten Bob found himself ducking behind a barricade of crates and wooden planks, as snowballs whizzed past him. He peeked over the top, only to be hit squarely in the chest by a perfectly aimed ball of snow. His attacker, CSM McBride, laughed heartily from a few yards away.

"Got yer, yer bugger!"

Not far from the snowball fray, a group of soldiers had taken to building snowmen. Their creations ranging from traditional figures with stick arms and coal eyes to more humorous constructs adorned with slouch hats and woollen scarves and gloves. One particularly impressive snowman stood tall with a steel helmet and a mock rifle, made from snow, its icy form bringing smiles to the faces of those who saw it.

Some of the more adventurous soldiers tried their hand at sliding down gentle slopes on makeshift sleds. Roo and Archie, always up for some excitement, found some flat pieces of wood and, with whoops of joy, pushed off from the top of a small hill, their mates cheering them on as they skidded and bumped their way to the bottom, leaving a trail of laughter in their wake.

Captain Ponsonby was fortunate enough to own a Kodak Box Brownie Camera and had been capturing events of the 9th Battalion since their time at Enoggera, so photographing these snowy scenes became a priority. Groups of soldiers posed with their snowmen, in the midst of snowball fights, and against the stunning white landscape, creating lasting mementos of this unusual and unforgettable time.

Yet, as the initial excitement waned, the challenges of the cold became apparent. The Australians, unused to such freezing conditions, huddling together; sharing whatever materials they could find to keep warm. Scarves, blankets, and bits of cloth were repurposed into makeshift insulation, and in the quiet moments between the play and the routine of military life, the men found themselves musing on the serene, untouched snow that contrasted so sharply with the devastation around them.

On the 5th of December Captain Ponsonby, in command of a scouting party, was sent out to an area known as 'Factory Corner' in order to familiarise themselves with their new positions. On their return journey they travelled via High Wood, behind which were sited some Australian 60 Pounder guns. As the group approached, a German barrage began to rain down around them, the shells falling closer and closer as branches of trees exploded before them sending splinters of wood in their direction. Then it landed; a sudden salvo of fire and metal engulfing the group of soldiers. Young Jacko, who was just to the front of Roo, went down immediately, dropping like a sack of potatoes, crumpling in a crimson pile of entrails, whilst the earth shaking explosion also knocked over Stowie and Ten Bob. Roo and Captain Ponsonby grabbed Jacko and ran with him to a safe, sheltered spot, about thirty yards away. Jacko was still alive but did not speak, passing out and moving on to the afterlife in a matter of minutes. Stowie and Ten Bob had been toppled by the percussion of the explosion and had been hit by shrapnel, but they appeared to be fine as they staggered to their feet, dazed and momentarily disorientated.

The air was now alive with bullets and artillery so Roo and Ponsonby laid poor Jacko gently down and, along with the rest of the party, moved out to safety. Before departing, Roo placed the palm of his left hand on Jacko's cold forehead, wiped the tears from his eyes and whispered, "We'll be back for you mate".

The next day Roo, Taff, Archie, Stowie, Clancy, Freddy, Sergeant Mac and the Padre went to the spot where poor Jacko lay and buried him; the seven mates returning the following day with a wooden cross which the Pioneers had made. Sergeant Mac, who had trained each of the men from the first day of their enlistment and 'helped' young Jacko aboard the troop ship at Pinkenba, was particularly choked up.

"I have no words for ye. Young wee Jackson here was a good lad...a good man, and a truly great soldier; as are ye all. I am proud to have known him and my heart feels a little empty now that one of our friends has left us," he said, trying to hold back the tears.

The rest of the group were hit hard by the loss of Jacko, but also by the unexpected emotion from Big Mac. As Mac hammered the cross into the earth, the group stood in silent vigil for their mate, with Roo managing to read out a final epitaph.

"Here lies our mate, in a spot that will forever be Australia".

On the 12th of December, the 9th Battalion, numbering nine hundred and thirteen men, was assigned as the support battalion to the 10th, which had just taken over the front line from the 12th Battalion. The 9th Battalion found their quarters in the remains of the village of Flers, now a desolate expanse of mud and ruins. 'B' Company took up position in Gap Trench, where they were greeted by a fresh blanket of snow on their first night, setting the tone for the nine days they would spend there.

The freezing air bit at their exposed skin as they settled in.

"Welcome to the winter wonderland of...where are we again...oh yeah, Flers," Clancy muttered, shaking the snow off his helmet.

"Could be worse," Roo said, trying to sound optimistic.

"Oh yeah? How?" Clancy asked.

"Well, at least it's not raining," laughed Roo.

Clancy chuckled and shook his head.

"Silly bugger".

On the 21st of December, the battalion moved to the front line. 'A' and 'B' Companies were positioned at the very front, with 'C' and 'D' Companies in close support within Smoke Trench. The two forward companies were separated by a gap of two hundred yards, with 'B' on the left of 'A'. These gaps were perilous during daylight hours and could only be crossed under the cover of night. Additionally, 'A' Company had another gap on its right flank, adding to the tension and the need for vigilance.

Patrolling was a harrowing ordeal, involving crawling through mud and enduring the biting cold. One night, as they slithered through the muck, Ten Bob turned to Taff and whispered, "You ever seen mud like this? It's like trying to swim through glue."

"Keep your voice down," Stowie hissed, his eyes scanning the foggy darkness, "the last thing we need is Fritz hearing us."

The relentless work on trench repairs was exhausting, as the sides, lacking proper support, frequently caved in. The weather compounded their misery, with fog and light misty rain adding to the chill. Temperatures often plummeted, turning the water and slush into treacherous ice.

On the 23rd of December, the front line companies began to be relieved on a daily basis. However, two days of heavy rain had transformed the landscape; shell holes now connected to form a vast marsh. Anyone attempting to walk across it risked sinking into mud and water up to their waist.

It seemed too that the continual alteration to the landscape in no man's land was resulting in soldiers losing their bearings. One particularly foggy night, Stowie and his section were on patrol when they heard muffled voices through the haze.

"Sounds like a carrying party with all that clanging," Stowie whispered.

"Could be ours *or* theirs," Taff replied, gripping his rifle tighter.

As they cautiously approached, they saw a group of soldiers stumbling through the fog.

"Hands up...er...hände hoch!" Stowie shouted, aiming his weapon.

The startled figures froze, and as the mist cleared, the section realised it was indeed a carrying party, but a German one from the 173rd Bavarian Regiment, hopelessly lost and now prisoners of war.

Back in the trench, Roo and Clancy were working on reinforcing a section of the wall.

"Think we'll get home by Christmas?" Roo asked, tongue in cheek, more to break the silence than out of hope.

Clancy shook his head.

"Hmmm," he replied, stroking his chin in thought, "it's the 25th in two days, so if we start walking we should be there in a couple of years...but in the mean time please accept this gift".

There was a wet splat as a snowball landed on Roo's head.

Roo laughed.

"Thanks mate...Merry Christmas".

"You too mate," Clancy replied with a wry smile.

To combat the freezing temperatures, two meals a day were sent to all locations; hot stew and tea, bread, butter, jam and cheese. Despite this, as the days wore on, the soldiers of the 9th Battalion continued to endure the harsh conditions, their mateship and determination becoming their most vital tools for survival, with each day, like Christmas Day, bringing new challenges.

The 25th of December 1916 was initially deemed a cleanup and repair day. Soldiers were set to fortify their positions, clear debris, and perhaps find a brief respite to celebrate the birth date of the man who, it was hoped, would be bring peace on earth and good will to all men. But on this day it was not to be, as, by order of Haig, disconnected from the brutality of the front line, every artillery piece in the 4th and 5th Armies fired on spots where the enemy was suspected of enjoying Christmas Day. The Germans retaliated of course with a fierce barrage that landed all along the line, falling on Smoke Trench, where some of the officers were in the midst of their Christmas dinner. The men, who had been hoping for a moment's peace, were thrust back into the maelstrom of war.

It was not only artillery in the game now as small arms and machine gun fire erupted from the enemy positions, mowing down men left and right who were unlucky enough to be in view. The once quiet trenches boiled over into chaos, as Stowie threw himself to the ground, narrowly avoiding the deadly hail of bullets.

"Get down! Keep low!" he yelled, his voice barely audible over the racket.

Muddy trenches caved in under the relentless bombardment, burying soldiers alive. Clancy and Roo, struggling to keep their heads down, witnessed the horrifying sight of their mates being torn apart by shards of red hot metal and bullets. As a shrapnel round exploded high above the line its steel rounds sprayed the trenches below, clanging off the steel helmets of the troops. Some of the rounds lost their momentum and dropped like marbles, whilst others hit the earth with force sending dirt and debris flying, at one point causing Archie to lose his balance and topple to the trench floor.

Taff looked across as Archie clambered to his feet.

"Hold on, Archie, you're hit!" Taff exclaimed, noticing the blood seeping through Archie's sleeve.

"It's just a scratch," Archie grunted, though his face betrayed the pain.

"Yes, well we need to get it checked out boyo," replied Taff.

Archie looked around at the explosive scene that enveloped them.

"Er...I think I can wait," he said.

"Keep your heads down, find some cover!" Clancy urged, pulling Roo down to the ground.

"Bloody hell, this is madness!" Roo shouted over the deafening blasts.

Clancy looked around at the exhausted faces of 'B' Company.

"All this...and for what? So the brass can show that we can ruin their Christmas bloody dinner?!" he muttered bitterly.

Roo, wiping the grime from his face, nodded.

"Yeah, and at what cost?"

"Bloody Haig doesn't care mate. He's miles away...bastard!" growled Clancy.

Despite the hundreds of rounds which had been fired, the bombardment yielded nothing. Haig's orders had resulted in death and destruction, leaving the men battered and disheartened. The shelling was renewed in the afternoon with Flers and surrounding areas being heavily bombarded, artillery shells raining down, turning the landscape into a hellish scene of destruction, compounding the day's casualties.

Many lives were lost that day, a reminder of the relentless and senseless nature of the war. The soldiers of the 9th Battalion, once again, found their resolve tested, their hope dimmed but not extinguished as they faced the wretched truth of their existence on the front lines.

As Clancy sipped on his hot tea he made a sarcastic toast.

"Merry bloody Christmas!"

Sadly the enemy artillery had not yet finished claiming the lives of 9th Battalion men with RSM Corfield falling foul of an enemy shell the next day.

On the 30th of December the Battalion was finally given a reprieve when it moved into Brigade Reserve at Bazentin Le Grande. Here they were allowed to rest and sleep whilst one hundred and nineteen partially trained reinforcements were used for fatigue duties.

In the nissen hut Captain Ponsonby sat at the head of the makeshift table, a weary but contented smile on his face. Around him, his men were sprawled on beds or perched on crates, enjoying the rare luxury of rest. Each man seemed older than their actual years, the dim light from the lanterns casting a soft glow on their faces, revealing lines etched by months of relentless fighting. Outside, the new reinforcements, still fresh and unscarred by battle, toiled with fatigue duties, their voices carrying faintly through the walls.

"It's good to finally get some proper rest," Roo remarked, his voice conveying a note of relief, "I can't remember the last time I had a sleep that wasn't interrupted by artillery".

"It feels like a different world here in Bazentin Le Grande," added Lieutenant Sargent, "only yesterday we were knee-deep in mud and blood, and now... a real roof over our heads".

Stowie nodded whilst rubbing his tired eyes.

"Those lads out *there* don't know how lucky they are. Fresh from Australia, not a clue about the hell we've seen."

"They'll learn soon enough," Clancy said, laughing bitterly, "no point in sugar coating it".

Roo sighed, looking at the new recruits outside.

"Still, I envy them a bit. They've got a clean slate; haven't been through what we have".

"Remember when we first got here?" Archie said, "We were just as keen, but at least we had Gallipoli under our belts."

"Aye boyo, Gallipoli was a different kind of hell," Taff said, "but it prepared us for what was to come".

"That was a lifetime ago," Captain Ponsonby interjected, "we've lost good men, and seen things that will haunt us forever. But we've also shown what we're made of. I'm proud of every single one of you".

There was a silent pause as the men took in the grateful words of their Captain.

"It's hard to believe we finally have a break," Taff remarked, as he looked over to Archie, "how's your arm by the way sarge?"

"Oh good thanks mate. The doc got the shrapnel balls out and all is well, see?" replied Archie, as he lifted his arm up and down.

"Jacko would have loved it here," Clancy said softly, his eyes distant.

A solemn silence fell over the group as they remembered their fallen mate. Jacko was a quietly spoken young man who on occasion was ready with a joke to lift their spirits even in the darkest times, and his loss was a wound that still felt fresh.

Big Sergeant Mac broke the silence, raising his tin cup.

"To Jacko...you wee beastie," he said, his voice steady but thick with emotion.

The others echoed the toast, their cups clinking together in a small, poignant tribute.

Clancy nodded; his expression grave.

"We'll never forget him, and the only way we can do him justice is by making it through this, together".

Roo raised his cup for a second toast.

"Here, here...good on yer Clance".

Taff, ever the optimist, grinned.

"Tonight, we sleep. Tomorrow, who knows?"

"And who bloody cares?" laughed Clancy.

As the men settled back into their beds, a feeling of calm settled over the group, and for the first time in months, they allowed themselves to believe that there might be a light at the end of the tunnel. The memory of Jacko and the sight of the new men reminded them why they fought, and for a moment, in the heart of Bazentin Le Grande, there was peace.

10

But not a drop to drink

For the lighthorsemen the extremely hot summer of 1916, the constant training, patrolling and battles, had rendered both men and horses thoroughly exhausted. Apart from their day in the city there had been no leave. Added to that, the as yet unfinished railway line and lack of transport had made the logistical supply train very slow. This had also affected the YMCA and the AIF canteens, which had been with the ANZACs from day one, resulting in the inability to vary the types of rations available to the men. Water was also in short supply, and often as rank as that in the wells at ANZAC the previous year.

Despite the setbacks of the supply chain, the men not only marvelled at, but were in awe of those in charge of logistical operations, and those who worked in that field. Indeed it was rare to hear the fighting troops being anything but grateful to the supply and support arms of the AIF and NZEF. Without ammunition, food, weapons, clothing, transport and engineering, the fighting men would be redundant.

The 15th of November had seen the 2nd Light Horse Regiment become part of the Desert Column, joining the ANZAC Mounted Division at Ge'Eila. The wonder of logistics was ever present, with the Egyptian Labour Corps having laid a mile of railway line per day, pushing it to Bir El Abd and Salmana. This enabled the Desert Column to assemble in rapid time, and with the now daily arrival by train of much needed supplies, the column was building up for its planned attack on Mazar, twelve miles away, where the Turks were now massing.

Along with the railway line, a fresh water pipeline had been constructed to carry filtered Nile water from the Kantara Canal to as far as Belah, and ensured that one hundred thousand men and thirty thousand horses were watered.

Protection of the column fell on the 1st Light Horse Brigade, with the regiments patrolling regularly and manning outposts, and pretty soon the Desert Column moved to Gererat, which was within striking distance of Mazar.

The Division deployed in its usual defensive position of two brigades on the front line, with the third in reserve; the horses being tethered in a scattered formation within easy reach of the troops, whilst being a difficult target for enemy aircraft.

In their bivouac area the men received an unexpected surprise.

"Boys! There's some pressies for you," announced Percy.

Christmas Billies for each man had arrived from the Regimental Comforts Fund Committee in Brisbane.

"Ripper!" exclaimed Chugger.

"The CO says a move is imminent so it's an early Christmas this year I'm afraid," said Percy.

"Early?" added Davo, "at least we're having one this year".

"What do you mean sarge?" asked a puzzled Johnno.

"He means eat the bloody stuff now yer dill, cos you can't take it with you," replied Chugger.

Before any future incursion in to enemy territory could be contemplated, the important question of whether it was possible to transport water to the advancing troops, was at the forefront of everyone's thoughts.

Captain Brown, with twenty troopers from 'C' Squadron, three engineers and a spear-head boring plant, were despatched to prospect for water in the Wadi El Arish, which was located well behind the Turkish lines. For communications they were equipped with a basket of carrier pigeons and a Helio; which was a signalling contraption which worked using mirrors like a Morse code type key, relaying signal messages across the landscape to other signalling stations.

The wadi was approximately thirty miles away and the trek

would be across very rough terrain, occupied by hostile Bedouins who were certain to provide intelligence to the enemy.

"Those pigeons looked tasty eh?" remarked Chugger as he had thoughts of pigeon pie.

"Keep your beady eyes off them mate," the signals sergeant responded, "if that Helio thing breaks, they are our only means of communication".

"Never mind the birds, if we don't find water we'll have nothing to drink until we get back," said a concerned Boggy.

As the body of men rode through the barren landscape they took note of important landmarks and possible ambush points, whilst avoiding enemy patrols. Upon arrival at the wadi the lighthorsemen dispersed in to interlocking defensive positions whilst the engineers drilled three unsuccessful bore holes.

"Bugger!" exclaimed Percy as he turned to Captain Brown, "what now sir?"

"Well, it is a bit of a disappointment, but we have gained some valuable intelligence about the lay of the land at least," replied the officer, "but we will pack up quickly and get the hell out of here I think".

"Good idea sir," said Percy, "as I'm sure our presence has not gone unnoticed".

Exhausted and thirsty, the prospecting patrol arrived back at the column after a thirty hour absence.

Reconnaissance patrols into enemy held territory continued, with the search for water a priority before any further advance could be made. Bedouin spies were everywhere and soon the

Turks received word of at least two allied patrols penetrating their lines, the alarm bells beginning to ring as to the safety of their positions at Mazar. Were these probes a sign of an imminent invasion by the British and those damned ANZACs? The Turks concluded that time may not be on their side, so an immediate withdrawal of all Turkish and German troops to El Arish was ordered.

This was a bad move by the enemy, for nothing escaped the ever vigilant eyes of British Intelligence, with General Chetwode ordering an all out advance on El Arish.

"How will we do that without water?" asked Johnno.

"I think you'll find that we will carry as much as we can, and travel via the Turks old possie at Mazar," replied Percy, "there's bound to be water there".

The advance was undertaken by the ANZAC Division (minus the 2nd Brigade) and the Camel Corps, who marched around El Arish during the night, whilst the Division's infantry battle groups proceeded directly by road, thus allowing them to arrive in a good state. But the Turks were aware of the ANZAC's plan to surround the town by first light, and knowing the endurance and stamina of the ANZAC horses, they and their German allies knew that their position at El Arish was a precarious one, so had decided to fly the coup just prior to the ANZAC division's arrival, making their way to the perceived security of Magdhaba.

Ever the optimist and wanting to strike whilst the iron was hot, General Chetwode decided on a surprise dawn attack of Magdhaba on the morning of the 23rd of December. The attack would be carried out by all of the division's mounted troops, which included the 1st, 3rd and New Zealand Mounted Rifle

Brigades, the Imperial Camel Corps, 18th Brigade Royal Horse Artillery and the Hong Kong and Singapore Mounted Battery. Despite the objective being twenty seven miles away, down a practically unknown and waterless track, this did not deter the Divisional Commander.

It was the 22nd of December and there was much organisation of ammunition, food and water to be done. But done it was.

That evening the advance on Magdhaba began, with 'C' Squadron acting as advance guard for the division, and as they pressed on through the inky blackness of the desert night, a sense of anticipation hung heavy in the air, the atmosphere charged with a mixture of excitement and apprehension, each soldier keenly aware of the impending battle that lay ahead.

The terrain was harsh and unforgiving, with undulating sand dunes stretching endlessly into the distance. The light from the Moon cast eerie shadows across the desert landscape, illuminating the silhouettes of men and horses as they moved stealthily forward, the only sound being the occasional whinny of horses and the muted voices of their mates, their whispered conversations carrying on the desert breeze.

Amidst the quiet murmurs, and the rhythmic thud of hooves against sand, thoughts of home inevitably surfaced. Some spoke of loved ones left behind, their voices tinged with longing and nostalgia, while others discussed what lay ahead, steeling themselves for the coming battle with words of encouragement and brotherhood.

"Oy, Davo, do ya reckon we'll catch those buggers off guard?" whispered Boggy, his voice tinged with a mix of excitement and nerves.

"Yeah, I reckon so," Davo replied, "we've got surprise on our side. Just keep your eyes peeled and your rifle ready".

Further back in the column, two friends whispered to each other as they rode side by side.

"You reckon we'll all make it through this one?" one asked quietly, concern lacing his words.

His companion shrugged; his expression grim.

"I hope so, mate. But you never know with these bloody battles. Just gotta keep our heads down and hope for the best".

Meanwhile Percy rode up and down the column whispering encouragement to the troops, his voice barely audible above the sound of hooves against sand.

"Keep your wits about you, boys, we'll give those bastards a run for their money".

Johnno responded in a hushed tone, his voice betraying a hint of uncertainty.

"I just hope we make it through in one piece. I can't bear the thought of never seeing home again."

"I can't bear the thought that this place we're going to probably won't have a pub mate," Chugger quietly laughed, his comment causing a ripple of muffled laughter through the ranks, "but we all have our crosses to bear eh?"

As they advanced through the desert night, there was also a sense of caution in the air, for every shadow, every rustle in the wind, held the potential for danger, the soldiers being acutely aware of the ever present threat of ambush, their senses heightened as they scanned left and right for any signs of movement.

Whispers among the men touched upon the possibility of

Bedouin spies lurking in the darkness, their eyes keen and their allegiance uncertain.

"Keep an eye out for any sign of trouble," one officer murmured, his words a reminder of the dangers that surrounded them, "we can't afford to let our guard down, not for a moment".

A trooper nodded in agreement, his grip tightening on the reins of his horse.

"Too right sir. Those Bedouin sure are crafty sods. We'll need to stay alert if we want to make it through this night".

And so, amidst the whispers of battle and thoughts of home, the mounted column rode steadily on, ever vigilant to the treacherous terrain of the desert, and of those who would seek to do them harm.

On arrival it was still dark and it was difficult to locate the Turkish positions as they had been expertly sited and concealed. 'C' Squadron dismounted and immediately fanned out, seeking sanctuary behind the many sand dunes.

"I can't see a bloody Abdul anywhere," said Boggy, as he passed his binoculars to Percy.

"Let's have a quick squizzy," said Percy, "someone or something is bound to give them away".

Magdhaba was yet another ancient town which had sat in the desert for centuries, undisturbed, and as Percy searched left to right, up and down, he could just make out the distant silhouettes of a mosque and the typical flat topped dwellings that existed in all Egyptian towns. But the Turks were sitting on the only water source for miles, so it needed to be taken. War had arrived in this peaceful town.

"This'll be like trying to take a bone from a dog," Percy whispered.

"Yeah. We'll definitely get bitten here I think," replied Boggy.

As Percy scanned the most likely ground for defensive positions, it was a dog which gave the Turks away as it suddenly appeared from out of the ground, hotly pursued by its owner...a Turkish soldier.

"Well bugger me!" Percy quietly exclaimed as he pointed to the prowling dog.

Boggy strained his eyes in the darkness, then smiled.

"And that's why you don't keep pets in the trenches eh?" Boggy noted, "poor bugger only wants to do his business".

"Yep, well thanks doggy," said Percy, "look, now that we have a start point to look at you can just about make out their positions. Do me a favour mate and go and grab Captain Stodart".

Boggy was soon back with the Captain, who quickly observed the ground to their front, a broad smile appearing on his face.

"Good work Sergeant Taylor...Marsh...I'll pass this on to Regimental Headquarters. Start preparing boys, I don't think we'll be long before the attack goes in".

"We're already set to go sir, just give us the word," replied Percy.

The attack was kicked off at 0630 hours by the Royal Flying Corps's 5th Wing who had dropped a hundred bombs on the town the previous day. They were now attacking the Turkish defences, strafing and bombing, in order to draw fire, thus revealing the enemy positions. There were a number of redoubts, encircling the village, which guarded the sole water source.

The Camel Brigade opened the ground attack, with the 2nd Brigade and the New Zealand Mounted Rifle Brigade on their left and the 1st Brigade on the right. The enemy position was practically enveloped by the division, and the Turks knew it. But, because they were an expert defensive fighter, especially when concealed behind cover, the attack was going to be harder than envisaged.

The primary assault of the Kiwis, originated from the north and east, and was carried out by advancing in orderly troop columns. They were supported by machine gun squadrons equipped with Vickers and Lewis guns, along with the 3rd Light Horse Brigade. The offensive commenced near Magdhaba village and Wadi El Arish, on the predominantly flat battleground. As British Empire artillery unleashed its barrage, the mounted troops manoeuvred towards the right and rear of the Ottoman garrison.

General Chauvel's envelopment strategy swiftly took shape. Despite intense Turkish resistance, the mounted troops sought shelter and dismounted, with some positioned approximately sixteen hundred yards from the enemy defences, while others ventured as close as four hundred yards. At the same time, units of the Imperial Camel Brigade advanced directly towards Magdhaba in a southeast direction, following along the telegraph line. By 0845 hours, they were steadily progressing on foot, followed by the 1st Light Horse Brigade held in reserve.

At approximately 0925 hours, the 10th Light Horse regiment was ordered to encircle the entrenched positions and move through Aulad Ali, their aim being to block potential routes of retreat to the south and southeast. The regiment, accompanied by two sections of the brigade Machine Gun Squadron, successfully seized Aulad Ali along with three hundred prisoners.

Locating the Turkish artillery batteries and trenches proved challenging. However, by 1000 hours, the New Zealand Mounted Rifle Brigade was moving closer to the firing line. Around this time, an aerial report noted the beginnings of a retreat among small groups of the Magdhaba garrison. Consequently, the still mounted reserve, the 1st Light Horse Brigade, received orders to advance directly towards the town, bypassing the dismounted Imperial Camel Brigade battalions. Despite facing severe shrapnel fire as they traversed the open plain, they sought refuge in the Wadi el Arish, dismounted, and resumed their advance against the Ottoman left at around 1030 hours.

Meanwhile, the battalions of the Imperial Camel Brigade continued their progression across the flat terrain, advancing section by section for nine hundred yards. Each section provided covering fire in turn, ensuring a methodical approach to their movement.

By noon, all brigades were deeply embroiled in combat. Simultaneously, the 3rd Light Horse Brigade's 10th Light Horse Regiment continued their encirclement manoeuvre around the garrison's right flank. An hour later, the right flank of the Imperial Camel Brigade battalions reached the 1st Light Horse Brigade and within fifty five minutes, intense fighting began to significantly impact the Turkish garrison, with persistent reports of small groups of Turkish troops retreating.

By 1415 hours, the 10th Light Horse Regiment pressed forward after securing Aulad Ali, traversing the Wadi el Arish and circling Hill 345 to assault the rear of Redoubt Number 4. By 1455 hours, the Imperial Camel Brigade's frontal assault approached within five hundred yards of the Turkish defences.

The men of the 2nd Light Horse Regiment at this stage were feeling quite dejected, as they had been detailed as reserve. However, the regiment was to have its day, thanks to the zeal of Major Markham.

Riding amongst the brigade like an excited Kangaroo, Major Markham, ably assisted by Major Chambers, quickly rallied anyone he could find from the brigade. As the officers approached 'C' Squadron, Boggy quickly piped up.

"What's going on sir?"

"We're attacking the enemy redoubt just over there...are you coming or not?" replied the Major.

"We're supposed to be in reserve sir, you know, just in case," Percy pointed out.

"Stuff that sarge. I think *just in case* has arrived, and besides we seem to have them on the run," announced Chambers.

Just as the boys were about to join the two Majors, Major Birbeck arrived excitedly on the scene.

"Come on 'C' Squadron, we need to cut off the Turkish retreat...follow me," he called out.

"Sorry Major Chambers," said Percy, "it looks like we have other places to be".

"Well, good luck to you," replied the Major as he touched the brim of his hat and gave a slight bow.

As the two Majors and their entourage, consisting of the 3rd Light Horse Regiment and three Troops of the 2nd Light Horse attacked the Turkish redoubt, Major Birbeck and his band of two Troops galloped wildly round to the rear of the Turkish position, threatening a mounted attack from the rear.

This unexpected show of strength was the straw that broke the camel's back. The defenders were beginning to falter and surrender in small groups. The 1st Light Horse Brigade had successfully seized Number 2 redoubt, and other buildings and additional redoubts on the left flank had also been captured. But once the dismounted Aussie and Kiwi attackers, bayonets fixed, had closed in within twenty yards, completely blocking the escape route for the enemy garrison, the Turkish commander, noting the serious gravity of their predicament, hastily hoisted a white flag and surrendered his entire force. Ten minutes later, the organised resistance came to an end, and with darkness creeping in, the sporadic gunfire gradually faded away. Prisoners were gathered, horses cared for, and the captured wells tapped for water.

On seeing this, the ANZACs felt a combination of disappointment and relief.

"Thank God for that," announced Boggy.

"Selfish bastards!" exclaimed Chugger, "I wanted to give it them back for Quinn's Post".

"I think there'll be plenty of other opportunities for that mate," replied Percy, "let's just be grateful that no more mates were lost today eh?"

There was some consolation in that Lieutenant Guiren and his Troop, from the 2nd Light Horse, were the first in to the town of Magdhaba, beating the 3rd Brigade by a whisker

Once the town had been secured, Chauvel entered Magdhaba and ordered the clearance of the battlefield.

As the allied soldiers lined up the captured Turkish and German soldiers, each side looked each other up and down. Whilst the Turks seemed very inquisitive about their captors, the German prisoners exuded arrogance.

"So these are the bastards we all signed up to fight then?" growled Chugger, "not as good as you think you are eh boys?"

The Germans made no reply.

"Bit of a surly bunch eh?" said Percy.

As the enemy soldiers piled up their weapons, souvenirs became rich pickings, especially Turkish bayonets. As for badges, buttons and insignia, the ANZACs bartered with the prisoners, handing over coins and any pieces of equipment that they could spare.

One Turk pointed at the Emu plumes which the lighthorsemen wore proudly in their slouch hats.

"Australia…what is this?" the man asked.

Chugger and Percy quickly glanced at each other, recalling the same question from a British soldier, and the answer they had given him.

Chugger winked at Percy.

"They are Kangaroo feathers mate," replied Chugger.

"Kangaroo feathers…" said the Turk, he and his mates seeming impressed and marvelling at the plumes, "very nice".

Another Turkish soldier appeared to be fixated on Percy, and in broken English he spoke.

"I know you Australia," he announced, as he stroked his chin in contemplation, "you were at Bomba Sirt".

"You must have me confused with someone else mate. I've never heard of Bomba Sirt, let alone been there," replied Percy.

"You were at Gallipoli...yes?" asked the Turk.

"We were mate. What of it?" Percy answered.

"Er...Bomba Sirt...er, how you say in English...bomb ridge?" said the Turk.

Percy shrugged his shoulders.

"High hill...where we were very close to each other," the Turk explained, "you bring my friend back to our trench, then later I throw over spice and cigarette, you throw bisküvi...um...biscuit".

Percy's eyes lit up as he recalled the incident at Quinn's Post.

"Bloody hell," responded Percy, as he shook the Turk's hand, "yes I remember, what are the chances? Pleased to see you again. I'm Percy and these blokes are Chugger, Boggy and Davo".

"I am Mehmet," the soldier replied, nodding in acknowledgement to all present.

"Hey, I seem to remember we tossed over a tin of bully and you threw it back," added Chugger.

Mehmet laughed.

"Yes. I remember. I very sorry".

"Hah...no need to be sorry mate. You probably thought we were trying to kill you with it," Chugger laughed.

Noticing that the line of surrendering soldiers was being held up by their conversation, Percy quickly jumped in.

"Listen Mehmet, we'll come and find you for a bit of a chin wag...er...talk, later. But I am glad you are safe now. No more war for you".

The Turkish and German force of over two thousand five

hundred men had either been killed or captured, and much useful equipment, stores and animals were seized.

The battle may have been won, but as ever, it was never a case of pack up and go home. The 1st Light Horse Regiment must have won the toss, for they were tasked with clearing the battlefield, which, although a gruesome task, enabled them to bivouac and catch up with some much needed sleep.

Having had little rest for eighty four hours, it was no surprise that the 2nd Light Horse had been detailed on a night escort of prisoners to El Arish. They were very disappointed.

"I reckon some bastard's got a double headed penny!" exclaimed Chugger, quite disdainfully.

"Too right mate," agreed Davo.

As it did not appear that Percy would have his promised chin wag, he quickly sought out Mehmet and managed to exchange addresses with him.

"Mind you keep in touch mate, and maybe we can meet up when all of this is over," said Percy.

"Perhaps I come to Australia one day," replied Mehmet.

The journey to El Arish was unpleasant, with some succumbing to fatigue and falling from their horses on to the sandy and rocky ground.

Thud!

"Bugger it!" Chugger groaned as he climbed to his feet and dusted himself off.

Percy tugged on his reins and turned to where Chugger's horse, George, was standing, looking lost and riderless.

"Come on Georgie. I bet you're tired too eh mate?" Percy whispered gently as he grasped the horse's bridle and trotted to where the slightly embarrassed Chugger stood.

"Are you right mate?" Percy asked.

"Yeah, I just fancied a stroll that's all," Chugger replied.

"I *bet* you did," chuckled Percy as he handed his mate the reins.

Even the Turkish prisoners thought the sight of Chugger falling quite comical, some giggling uncontrollably.

As Chugger placed his foot in the stirrup and hauled himself back in to the saddle he glared at the prisoners.

"Yeah...righto. What are you cheeky buggers laughing at?" he growled as he eyed the Turks up and down, "the war is over for you blokes. Do you get it?"

"Yes...thank you," responded one of the Turks.

Chugger then realised the gravity of his last comment.

"Bloody hell...yeah I think I'd be laughing too boys; good on yer".

The regiment managed a rest stop at Lafan, half way to El Arish.

"Dinner time boys. Break out the Bully," said Percy.

Only a few of the Turkish prisoners had rations and water, so the Aussies shared what they had with their former foe.

"Well, it's either that or eat behind a sand dune eh?" said Boggy.

As the Turks gobbled up the Bully Beef, Percy remarked, "they've changed their tune since Gallipoli eh?"

"Amazing what hunger does to a man," replied Davo.

The convoy of Light Horse, and prisoners, arrived at their destination at dawn on Christmas Eve. El Arish was some distance from the railway line so rations were in short supply. The prisoners were passed to the Scots of the 52nd Division who were annoyed because they now had to share *their* food with the captured Turks, thus going short themselves; the disgruntled Scots pointing out to the Aussies that they had taken far too many prisoners and should have made more use of the bayonet.

The reward in the end for the Aussies was rain and, yet again, no tents.

"It's flamin' Egypt all over again!" announced Chugger.

"Yeah. Happy bleedin' Christmas one and all," added Boggy.

There was no Christmas dinner as such, with rations being the fayre of the day, and the only gifts were the chance to catch up with some much needed sleep.

Rafa and Weli Sheikh Nuran were situated twenty one and twenty eight miles, respectively, from the brigade's current position, and they were both very strong posts which could still threaten the Suez Canal.

As it transpired, there certainly was no let up for the 2nd Light Horse who, along with the rest of the 1st Light Horse Brigade, were despatched as a recce group on the 30th of December 1916, arriving at Sheikh Zowaiid just before sunset. From there the Brigade Commander and his escort used the cover of darkness to recce the area around Magruntein, approximately two and a half miles south west of Rafa. Here is where the enemy force of around one thousand was located. The brigade, it seemed, was used as a huge escort for the brigade staff to carry out the recce, but did manage a few hours rest at Sheikh Zowaiid as they shivered their way through one of the coldest nights that they would ever experience.

"This place is colder than winter on Gallipoli boys!" exclaimed Percy.

"Too right, and it was brass monkey weather there," replied Boggy.

Just before dawn, when the warmth of the sun was about to bring comfort to the men, the brigade was quietly roused and, in quick fashion, set off on their journey back to El Arish.

Boggy glanced around the arid terrain, which was still cloaked in the final shadows of the night.

"I'm surprised we haven't seen hide nor hair of Turkish patrols boys," he uttered quietly.

"The Turks don't need to find us," replied Chugger as he gazed around at the Bedouin pedlars who followed the columns of soldiers everywhere, "these bastards are your mates when you hand over a few shillings, but you can bet that they spill their guts to old Jacko at every chance they get".

As Chugger spoke, a pedlar pushed some of his wares in his face.

"You want eggs a cook Australia?"

"Get away from me yer mug or I'll drop yer," Chugger growled as he slapped the Arab's hands away.

Following the recce, Major General Chetwode, the overall commander, issued orders to attack Magruntein. The mounted troops of the Desert Column, plus the 5th Cavalry Brigade, were tasked with the attack, ably assisted by artillery units from the Inverness and Ayrshire Batteries, the Royal Horse Artillery, the

Somersets, the Honourable Artillery Company, and the Hong Kong and Singapore Mountain Batteries.

At 1700 hours on the 8th of January 1917 the column moved out. Marching all night, they were able to surround the position from south to east before the sun rose. Attacking from the north, the 1st Brigade were the first in to action, with the Camel Corps and Yeomanry attacking from the east and south respectively. The 3rd Brigade was sent in between the Camel Corps and the 1st Brigade, their 8th Light Horse Regiment being sent to observe and intercept any enemy force which may come from the direction of We'Li Sheikh Nuran. At 0900 hours the 1st and 2nd Light Horse were ordered in first, with the 3rd Light Horse acting as brigade reserve. The enemy artillery had a perfect field of fire, but, by excellent observation the light horse regiments managed to locate a road which ran parallel with their advancing line, and was sunken, affording them valuable cover from enemy artillery and small arms fire.

The lighthorsemen dismounted and now lay on the top edges of the sunken road, sending down a harassing fire, hoping to gain fire superiority, whilst allowing friendly artillery to take up fire positions in order to knock out the well sited and accurate enemy guns.

"It's just like the charge of the light brigade," Percy shouted over the noise of the rifle fire.

"Eh?" asked Chugger.

"You know…Turkish guns to the left and right?" replied Percy.

"What *are* you flamin' going on about sarge?!" exclaimed Chugger.

"Never mind," replied a disappointed Percy as he whispered to himself, "bloody heathen".

"Now that one I heard!" Chugger piped up.

"Just keep firing mate," said Percy, "and let's hope the Kiwi brigade gets here soon".

The travelling distance for the New Zealand Mounted Rifle Brigade had been grossly underestimated but, eventually, they appeared and formed up on the 1st Brigade's right. It seemed that the attack plan had been hastily devised and there was a distinct lack of co-ordination between units. Like the 1st Light Horse Brigade, the Camel Corps were getting severely knocked about, and the Yeomanry had been forced to withdraw. By 1700 hours no progress had been made, and a substantial enemy force was believed to be advancing from the north.

The situation at first sight seemed critical and Chetwode was under the impression that he had been defeated, sending orders to each brigade to withdraw.

"What?!" exclaimed Boggy, "I aint pulling back. What about the wounded?"

"Bloody oath mate," agreed Chugger.

Just then Percy noticed movement on their right flank.

"Look boys, the Kiwis are advancing on foot with their bayonets fixed".

The New Zealand Mounted Rifle Brigade had clearly not received the orders to withdraw, and saw an opportunity and took it.

Percy could see that the 1st and 2nd were itching to go forward and, catching the eye of Captain Stodart, shouted "what do you reckon sir, shall we join our Kiwi mates?"

The officer, seeing the positives in the situation, gave Percy the nod and both men yelled to all in earshot to fix bayonets and advance in extended line towards the town.

"About time boys!" Davo shouted to his mates.

The two brigades of ANZACs moved as one, bayonets glistening in the fading sunlight. A few Turks, fearing the cold steel of the advancing enemy, were terrified and immediately threw up their hands. The 2nd Light Horse Regiment's field telephone was the only one in the line still operating, thanks to Lieutenant Letch and Signaller Mercer, who had worked tirelessly under fire throughout the day, repairing the line. It was because of this that the ANZAC advance was relayed up the chain of command, the withdrawal cancelled and a general advance ordered. The advance was a complete success with the guns and the enemy falling silent.

With no risk of enemy re-enforcements, clearing up the battlefield and caring for the wounded was a long one.

The 8th Light Horse Regiment took on the role of rear party whilst the 2nd and the remainder of the troops departed for Sheikh Zowaiid just after midnight. On arrival, all except the sentries and OPs managed a few hours of much needed sleep.

Following stand to the next morning there was much discussion around breakfast campfires about the attack and the way it was handled.

"Good on the Kiwis for pressing the attack," announced Davo.

"I think it is more like good on the commander for his poor decisions and communication," responded Percy.

"How so?" asked Chugger as he pierced his bully beef tin with his bayonet.

"Well, it was a stuff up from the start," said Percy, "like our mate Davo here said a while back, the British just don't know what to do with us and the Kiwis, or *how* to use us".

"I don't know, it all worked out in the end didn't it?" said Boggy.

"Yeah, but at what cost though?" said Percy, "from what I can see the Jackos didn't even know we were there. We could have galloped in and dismounted under cover of darkness and it would have been all over in fifteen or twenty minutes".

"And probably with less casualties," added Chugger.

"Don't forget that the Turks really fear the bayonet; well who doesn't I suppose," said Percy, "so a quick bayonet advance in the dark would have settled the matter quick smart".

"You should mention this to our officers. Maybe they can pass it up the chain," suggested Davo.

"Maybe I'll give it a go boys," replied Percy.

"Good on yer sarge; now get some of this into yer," said Chugger, tossing a bully beef tin towards his mate.

Eleven men had died in the attack and another eight were wounded.

The Turks, if they hadn't learned in 1915, were soon aware of the ferocity and tenacity of the ANZAC mounted troops and their regular patrols, so withdrew all troops from their outposts to the Gaza-Beersheba line. With its increasing strength it was fast becoming a formidable position and obstacle to future advances.

The 2nd Light Horse was in need of a rest, but the brigade

staff seemed to have no idea or thought to this and, accordingly, ordered the regiment to relieve the 2nd Brigade of their line communication work at Mazar. On arrival, 'C' Squadron was sent to Malha. Here they carried out musketry training plus other tactical and field training, utilising experiences from their most recent battles; so someone was *indeed* listening. As well as training, they were sent out on regular patrols of the water pipeline.

In March 1917 the regiment moved to Hill 200, near El Arish, holding posts along the wadi to Lahfan, plus patrolling to Magdhaba, to protect the right rear of the main force which was scheduled to attack Gaza.

Although 1917 had arrived, the Taylor boys would never forget the events of 1916. The 9th Battalion started the year by garrisoning the Suez Canal at Gebel Habeita before moving on to France and Flanders. They had taken part in the raid at Fleurbaix, fought in the battles of Pozieres and Mouquet Farm, and after a period of rest at Ypres, joined the first battle of the Somme. As for the 2nd Light Horse Regiment they had spent their year in the blistering desert heat patrolling, scouting, protecting water supplies and railway lines, not to mention taking part in the battles of Romani, Magdhaba and Magruntein. Whilst the 9th Battalion were resting and training in Europe, the 2nd Light Horse Regiment had sat out the first battle of Gaza on the 26th of March, which was a defeat, but the 6th of April saw them, along with the brigade, marching to Khan Yunis, where the column was assembling for the second attack on Gaza.

It was not only the battles that would remain etched in each man's mind, but the loss of so many mates, including Private Jackson, who had been with the boys of the 9th Battalion from the start, not only surviving his feared ocean journey to Egypt but fighting for seven months at Gallipoli, then taking part in the savage battles around Pozieres, only to be killed by an artillery shell at Factory Corner. He was a good soldier and an even better mate, and was sadly missed.

1916 was just the beginning for the 9th Battalion with battles at the Maze, Lagnicourt, Bullecourt and Passchendaele still to come. As for the 2nd Light Horse Regiment, they were now in Palestine. There are battles still to be fought and won, so Percy, Archie, Roo and their mates will march again.

Tony Squire, originally from England, is now an Australian citizen and resides there with his wife Sheila. Following in his father's footsteps, he pursued a career as a professional soldier and dedicated a total of 21 years to his service. Throughout his life, he has held a deep passion for history, particularly military history, and from a young age, he aspired to craft a historical novel that would intertwine his characters with real life historical events. This dream has come to fruition multiple times through his books aimed at younger readers, featuring his beloved character Buckley the Yowie. However, in his latest endeavours, novels intended for adult readers, Tony has embarked on his long awaited journey of chronicling the remarkable tales of the ANZACs during the tumultuous period of the Great War.

More Books By This Author

IN THE COMPANY OF OUTLAWS - MY LIFE WITH NED KELLY AND HIS GANG.

The ANZAC Chronicles:

"...UNTIL YOU ARE SAFE".

Milton Keynes UK
Ingram Content Group UK Ltd.
UKHW021118070624
443893UK00014B/748